THRIVING IN THE ECONOMIC TSUNAMI

THRIVING IN THE ECONOMIC TSUNAMI

Kirk Elliott, PhD

© 2022 Kirk Elliott, PhD

ISBN
Paper: 979-8-218-11030-7
Kindle: 979-8-218-11031-4

Kirk Elliott PhD Private Advisors
1660 17th Street, Suite 400, Denver, CO 80202

www.kirkelliottphd.com

Cover design by Chris Taylor, www.SeraphimChris.com
Typography by **documen**. www.documen.co.uk
Printed in the USA

ABOUT THE AUTHOR

Dr. Kirk Elliott is the Founder and Chief Visionary Officer of Kirk Elliott PhD Private Advisors, an investment advisory firm specializing in tangible assets and serving a global clientele. The philosophy of the firm is People over Profit. As part of that the firm gives a portion of its revenue to partner with non-profits involved in anti-sex trafficking, poverty, and human restoration. Kirk lives in downtown Denver with his wife, 17-year-old son, and a CavaPoo named Ted.

EDUCATION

Th.D. Theology, Phoenix University of Theology

Ph.D. Public Policy and Administration, Walden University

M.A. International Studies, University of Denver, Josef Korbel School of International Studies

B.S. Business Administration, University of Colorado

PROJECTS

- Engaging a Culture in Conflict (2018)
- Comparative Analysis of Inflation Adjusted Investment Returns 2000-2017 (2017)
- Strategic Investing (2017)
- How Nations Die | Lessons from History: The Fall of Rome and America Today (2017)
- Co-creator and producer of The Missing Chapter Curriculum (2015)
- 300 Million Slaves (2013)
- 10 Ways to Avoid the Economic Tsunami (2013)
- Surviving Global Governance (2013)
- The Gold and Silver Mastery Program Curriculum (2013)
- An Empirical Identification of an Appropriate Inflation Definition and an Inflation Targeting Monetary Policy Regime (2007)

PUBLICATIONS

(2018) *Engaging the culture in a time of conflict.* Elliott Global: Durango, CO.

(2018) *Comparing economic policy: strong dollar vs. weak dollar.* Elliott Global: Durango, CO.

(2018) *Current economic analysis: strategies for 2018.* Elliott Global: Durango, CO.

(2017) Becoming a Family of World Changers in Silk, D. (Ed.), *Parenting with purpose* (pp. 29-33). Retrieved from http://books.noisetrade.com/ dannysilk/parenting-with-purpose?download=1

(2017) *Strategic investing.* Sovereign Advisors: Colorado Springs, CO.

(2015-2016) *The missing chapter curriculum.* Wisdom Safari: Durango, CO.

(2014) *300 million slaves: America and its "free" society.* Today's America: Durango, CO.

(2013) *300 million slaves documentary: America and its "free" society.* Today's America: Durango, CO.

(2013) *The gold and silver mastery program.* Access Media: Colorado Springs, CO.

(2013) Ten ways to avoid the economic tsunami. Today's America: Durango, CO.

(2007) *An empirical identification of an appropriate inflation definition and an inflation-targeting monetary policy.* Today's America: Durango, CO

(1994) *The trend towards a unified global system: The changing political, economic, and social structures that are moving towards a new world order.* Unpublished Masters Thesis, University of Denver, Denver, Colorado.

CONTENTS

CHAPTER 1

THE TWO MILLION DOLLAR CUP OF COFFEE

SEXAGINTUPLE VANILLA BEAN MOCHA FRAPPUCCHINO

128 ounce glass with 60 shots of espresso!!!!

$54.75

K·E

While that extra-large Frappuccino® is obviously a group drink—or a crazy person's order—five days per week a twenty-year-old friend of the family was in the habit of driving forty miles round trip to get her normal-sized Frappuccino and a pastry. Not even accounting for gas or the pastry, let's assume she spent $4.25 per day. With twenty-two weekdays in an average month, her expense was $93.50 per month.

Now let's look at the average American millionaire: they do not look, dress, eat, or act like millionaires. They don't have millionaire names. They do live well below their means, wear inexpensive clothes, save, drive American cars, and invest what they do not spend. About two-thirds of American millionaires work (most are self-employed).

Next, let's take a quick look at some major asset trends in US history:

1. From 1980 to 2000 the DJIA grew 1404%, an average annual rate of 14.5%.

2. From 1970 to 2000, US real estate prices grew 593% (10.7% annually).

3. For the decade of the 1980s, US bonds averaged 9.46% per year.

4. From 2002–2014, gold grew from $278 to $1230 per ounce, a 342% increase in 14 years, or 13.1% per year on average.

Getting back to our daily-Frappuccino friend, if she quit the coffee run and invested that $93.50 at a 12% annual growth rate, what would she have at retirement? From age 20 to 65, how much would she have saved by investing her $4.25 per day? Would it be $10,000, $50,000, or maybe even $100,000? Actually, she would have much, much more! Even with no increased contribution because of inflation, by retirement she would have over $2 million dollars.

STRATEGY AND BUDGETING FOR SUCCESS

Now replace our Frapp friend with yourself: what is your "coffee"? Where can you save? Eating out? Satellite or cable television? Gadgets? Snacks? Sodas? The list of possible savings is extensive. Learn to live below your means, find fun activities that are free, invest in the right trend at the right time, learn how to budget, and stick to your plan. Those simple steps *will* help you live below your means, save up for the more expensive items you want to purchase, allow you more money to give away, and give you a comfortable retirement.

THE FORMULA FOR SUCCESS: 70-10-10-10

From any and all income, always immediately take 10% off the top and give it to a person or group that is either helping God's kingdom or performing some sort of good that you can financially assist with. Give steadily because not only it is the right thing to do, but the habit usually also brings more back to you in the long run. On the other hand, stingy people often end up living paycheck to paycheck. Instead, give the first 10% of your income because it is the "first fruits" of your labor—give your best. If you wait until everything else is allocated, you often have nothing left to give. Rather than wait to give until you have some future abundance, learn to give out of your need and desire to be a giver—it will change your life!

Next, allocate 70% of your income for living expenses: bills, car and house or rent payment, insurance, food, cloths, entertainment, and so on.

Then save 10% for the items you want to purchase in the near to intermediate future.

Invest the last 10% for retirement, and do not touch any of it until that time.

We maintain our individual freedom by building a solid foundation of giving and remaining debt free. For those who owe, make a commitment today to *declare war* on your debt!

CHAPTER 2

IDENTIFYING THE ENDGAME: A RESET IS COMING

A lie can stay hidden for a while, but never forever; the truth will always be exposed. As an example, many Americans finance a house or car through their bank, and also throw nice clothes, jewelry, and vacations on one of their many credit cards. When their current spending power reaches its limit, they eventually cave to applying for another, maybe to help put their teen into college, get a second car, head out to eat, or when the thought of another family trip becomes an obsession. The potential list of reasons to seek new debt goes on and on.

All that works okay until credit card and bank payments become too much for the family's income. Now what? Get a second job? Sell stuff? The last one normally means a loss on the original purchase price. People can always attempt to refinance higher-rate credit cards for a lower rate, sometimes even with zero interest for a while or no payments for six months, maybe even get a better rate with a second mortgage that pays off the charge cards. Phew! Crisis averted! That is, until they attempt a third and fourth mortgage, or apply for the seventh credit card, after which they receive this sort of disappointing letter:

"Your application has been denied. You have too much revolving debt on your credit report."

Now what, file for bankruptcy? Yikes, that means no more credit cards for a while, except at crazy-high interest rates. And this sort of financial status makes it almost impossible to refinance a house. The façade ends. What are their friends, family, and neighbors going to think? With all the nice things bought on bank loans, credit cards, and other financing, everyone thought they were successful, conquering the world and living an amazing life. But now the game is over, the years of hidden truth are out in the open, and the lies have been exposed. And it is painful, affecting their health, sleep, relationships, and reputation.

Does this story sound familiar? It should. This is how most of the American economy was built—on a bed of lies, a concocted false reality, a disguise. There are a few morals to this story:

1. A borrower is a slave to the lender. There is no freedom in debt.

2. The piper must always be paid.

3. When living a lie, life is great until the inevitable moment that it is not.

Even one of history's most famous authors filed for bankruptcy. But how could this have happened to a prolific bookseller like Ernest Hemingway? For him and everyone else, the answer is simple: Living your life above your means for very long will always result in you running out of money and possibly having to file for bankruptcy, which earns you a scarlet letter, a tarnished reputation that makes for a difficult pathway just to get near starting over. When Ernest was asked how his bankruptcy happened, the answer matched this common scenario mentioned above:

"It started slowly and then just happened."

Again, given enough time (and often when you least expect it), living a lie will *always* catch up with you.

Exactly the same precarious position—of potentially falling into an inescapable financial pit at any moment—is what most every nation on earth is in right now, all with the same sort of economic system as America, one built on debt extended by private central banks. And who are the owners of those behemoth banks? Well, why do you think some estimates put today's Rothschild, banking family and their central-banking fortune at around $300 *trillion*? While on that subject, why aren't they and the rest of the planet's trillionaires placed on *Forbes* magazine's yearly list of the 500 richest people in the world? Isn't that strange? Another lie? Yes.

Getting back to America's finances, the only reason we haven't yet filed for bankruptcy is that the US dollar has a unique position as the world's only reserve currency, meaning all international settlements are paid for in our central bank's Federal Reserve notes. So, there is enormous built-in demand, meaning the Fed can print without discretion to satisfy the international desire for their currency.

But just like our dismal scenario about overspending families, no matter what the situation or however dominant were any of history's unbacked (unsupported by any tangible asset like gold, silver, or oil) paper currencies, not one has stood the test of time. Under the increasing weight of debt, they always fail. Now, this does not mean those societies cease to exist, only that their finances are going to change, and the transition *will* be catastrophic. In America's case, imagine how impossible a peaceful and easy transition will be when it involves the reserve currency in the world's largest economy. Either way, an end is coming and it will include a necessary *reset*.

With the knowledge and warning of those monumental consequences, how might we know when our own currency game is about over? Well, we must understand where to look. Luckily, today there is no need to speculate because the signs are happening right under our noses. This is a bit complicated, but I will explain in more detail after giving you the full picture: Our first consideration is any potential *liquidity crisis* (lack of needed funds) within the banking system. Another gauge simply involves fundamental forces that can cause a *financial market collapse*. And the third is a function of the directives (missions) given to the Federal Reserve with regard to *interest rates*.

So signs that our currency is at its end will be noticeable from any liquidity crisis, impending market collapse, or the Fed's handling of interest rates, each of which we will look at more in the sections below.

Any one of those three can quickly obliterate the current US economic system, and these are certainly the same fundamental issues facing the global economy, which will ravage the world and cause shocking financial damage that will require a complete overhaul—a global reset. I predict that the only way to restore accountability, transparency, and stability to the system will be to bring about a new gold-backed, global currency that revolves around a reliable quantum financial system.

Again, how do we know our present central bank's unbacked paper-currency system is about to break? Speculation is unnecessary because we can easily identify current trends and issues that are right out in the open, and the policies we see from governments testify to the fact that we are nearing the end of this current currency system that has controlled the global economy for centuries. In more detail, let's consider these policy initiatives and trends that amplify my point:

BANKS ARE ON THE VERGE OF A LIQUIDITY CRISIS

On December 20th, 2020, the Federal Reserve issued a memorandum that required fifteen international banks with US operations to submit (by December 17th of 2021) an "Orderly Resolution Plan" to the United States *Bankruptcy Court*! As you can see, this directive gave banks one year to show how they would deal with a liquidity crisis. Words have real meaning, so let's dissect the reason for that memorandum, which will give us a laser focus on the crucial issue: What is an "orderly resolution"? *Orderly* means a systematic, non-chaotic outcome, and *resolution* involves resolving (fixing) something broken. And who are the recipients of this directive? They are these fifteen banks that the memorandum identifies as needing to submit this orderly resolution plan:

1. Barclays
2. Bank of Montreal
3. BNP Paribas
4. Capital One Financial Corporation
5. Credit Suisse
6. Deutsche Bank
7. HSBC Holdings plc
8. Mizuho Financial Group, Inc.
9. Mitsubishi UFJ Financial Group, Inc.
10. Northern Trust Corporation
11. The PNC Financial Services Group, Inc.
12. Sumitomo Mitsui Financial Group, Inc.
13. The Toronto-Dominion Bank
14. UBS
15. U.S. Bancorp

Do you think that means the Fed believes these entities are on the verge of bankruptcy and insolvency? Since the second part mentions the *US Bankruptcy Code,* the most likely answer is yes. What did the Fed see happening after December of 2021 that caused them (a year earlier) to write a 98-page memorandum focused on potential bankruptcies, and does that parallel with the massive debt spiral and inflationary pressures we are now seeing in America? With all our nation's financial troubles, it's no wonder banks have been facing liquidity issues, and this memorandum from Christmas of 2020 shows how increasingly nasty our country's finances have gotten.

And how did they know? No one has that clear of a crystal ball, so we can infer that the Fed may have known their decades of ill-advised policies had created the foundation for these banks and the rest of the global economic system to meltdown. Or, they may have purposely been working their master plan to bring the world's finances into such chaos that people will excuse their massive corruption. Reeling from a financial crisis, people tend to beg and scream for any kind of fix—a return to normalcy—which is just what the money printers want so that they end up paying no price for their malfeasance. And their pre-planned cure for the economic mayhem they caused will surely keep the vast majority of mankind as their indentured servants, a new system that will likely require the same or more of the people's labor, but with even less money and freedom for those not in their elitist club—just ratcheted-up fascist control.

This may sound extreme, but the first step in dismantling the current system is to eliminate private banking, with its saturation of money lenders who charge usury (unreasonable) rates. Starving the private banks of capital causes average people to bypass private-sector banks, going directly to government for capital and support.[1]

WE SEE FURTHER EVIDENCE OF A LIQUIDITY CRISIS IN THE REVERSE REPO MARKET

A reverse repo, or "reverse repurchase agreement," is a mechanism where banks make short-term, guaranteed loans (even just overnight) to central banks like our Federal Reserve. The utilization of these transactions is a sign of excess liquidity in the system, meaning banks have money left over, even after accounting for what they lend, invest, or hold against liabilities. The mechanics of a reverse repo involve a bank giving the Federal Reserve cash in exchange for US Treasury bonds (often called *Treasuries* for short). Generally in an economic crisis, the opposite transaction happens: Banks receive cash from central banks like the Fed, so they can lend it out, attempting to stimulate the economy. With the *reverse repo*, cash from banks goes into central banks in exchange for Treasuries, so it drains the amount they have to lend to consumers and businesses for operating capital and expansion—wealth-producing, economy-supporting activities.

With that in mind, what happened with reverse repos in 2021 defies logic. Consider the following two charts that show how 2021 saw a massive ramping up of reverse repos—huge quantities of cash leaving the banks to go into central banks like no other time in US history:

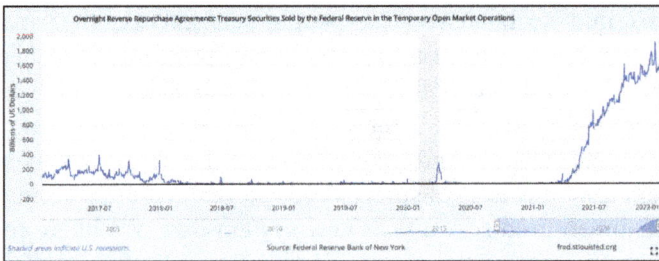

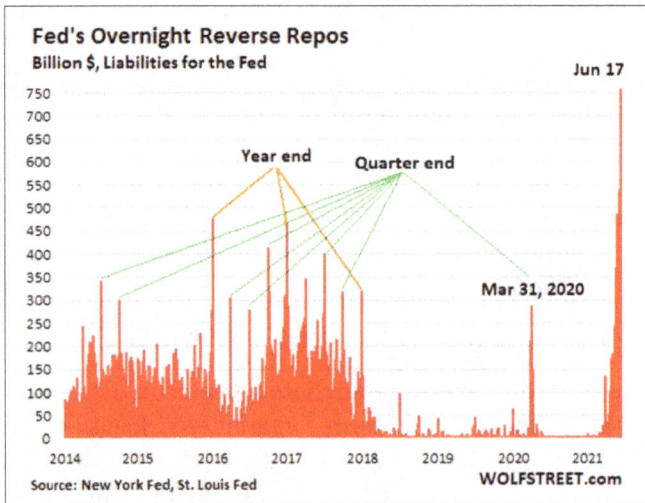

In 2021, during a time the US economy had been struggling from Covid lockdowns—when banks needed liquidity the most to lend out for help stimulating growth—the Fed had been removing mountains of cash from the system. This left banks handcuffed, consumers and businesses left out to dry with no available cash or credit, while the Federal Reserve bled US Treasuries off their balance sheet. In the December 2021 FOMC (Federal Open Market Committee) meeting notes, the Fed disclosed 2022 plans to continue pushing their US Treasuries into banks. As evidence that they are carrying through, consider the following chart showing how that process has continued to quickly change the Fed's balance sheet:

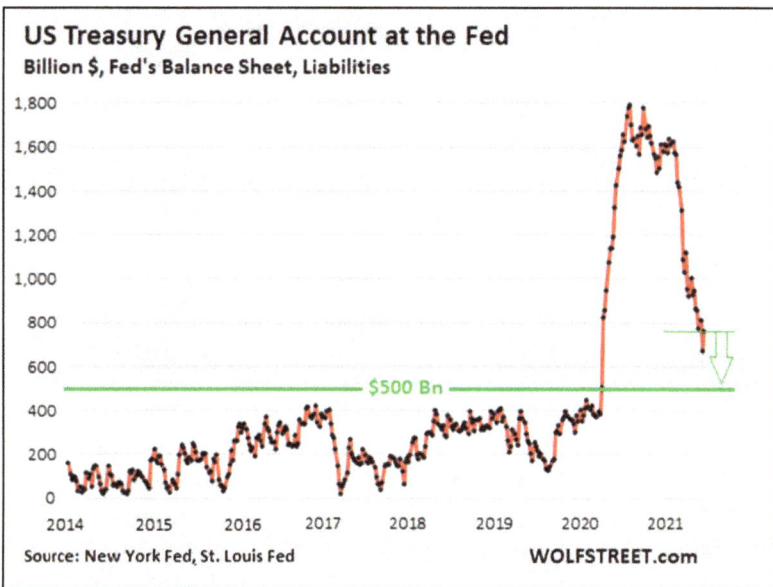

US Treasury General Account at the Fed
Billion $, Fed's Balance Sheet, Liabilities

Source: New York Fed, St. Louis Fed   WOLFSTREET.com

Again, what core assets has the privately owned Federal Reserve been accumulating over the years from all their money printing of loans to the American people, in the form of US dollar promissory notes? Most of what they gained have been US Treasury bonds—claims on the assets of the United States. While almost the entire globe has stopped purchasing US Treasuries, now the largest purchaser from the past many years, the Federal Reserve, has also ended their purchases. So, today we see a world with *no demand* for our US Treasury bonds. It had increasingly been the Fed who picked up the slack from other nations no longer acquiring US

Treasuries. Consider this chart showing how Treasury purchases by the Fed had been greatly accelerating to record levels, as global demand for the Fed's greenbacks was all but vanishing:

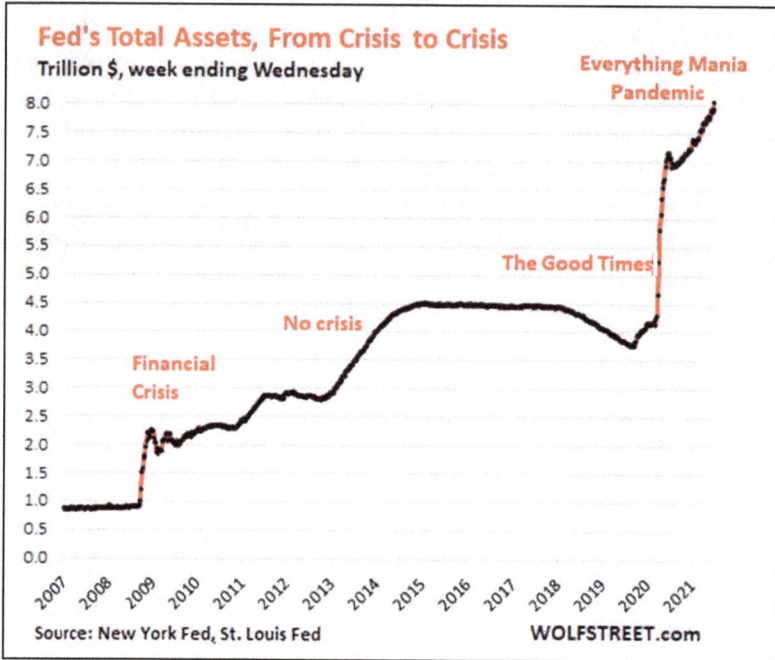

Fed's Total Assets, From Crisis to Crisis
Trillion $, week ending Wednesday
Source: New York Fed, St. Louis Fed   WOLFSTREET.com

This leaves the private central banking cartel (the Fed) with no other path but to increasingly inflate the money supply—print, print, print—or die. They produce more paper currency without discretion, manufacturing Federal Reserve notes with reckless abandon, just to keep the US economy afloat. Can you see why we are experiencing monstrous inflation in America? There is a problem here: The Fed is pulling money out of the banking system, leaving those banks with a liquidity issue. If the Fed is stopping its asset-purchase program (buying US Treasuries), why would they have to inflate or die? The simply answer is direct payments to US citizens via stimulus and other bailouts. But the result is just a bandage; they did nothing to heal the wound—they only temporarily covered it up, not allowing it to properly heal.[2, 3]

A MASSIVE SLOWDOWN IN GLOBAL MANUFACTURING

One of the most accurate leading indicators of any global-production slowdown is the Baltic Dry Index (BDI), which details the cost of shipping major raw materials. BDI tracks the price for moving goods from around the world and makes a reliable barometer (from world economic authorities) because it's composed of real-time updates—without speculation.

The index shows a low or high number, depending on whether demand for raw manufacturing materials is relatively little or a lot. Looking at this next chart, you can see that the Baltic Dry Index cratered in the last quarter of 2021, meaning global demand for raw materials was simply not there as we go into what appears to be a 2022 blood bath for stock and bond markets because the forecast for global sales of finished goods is not good.[4]

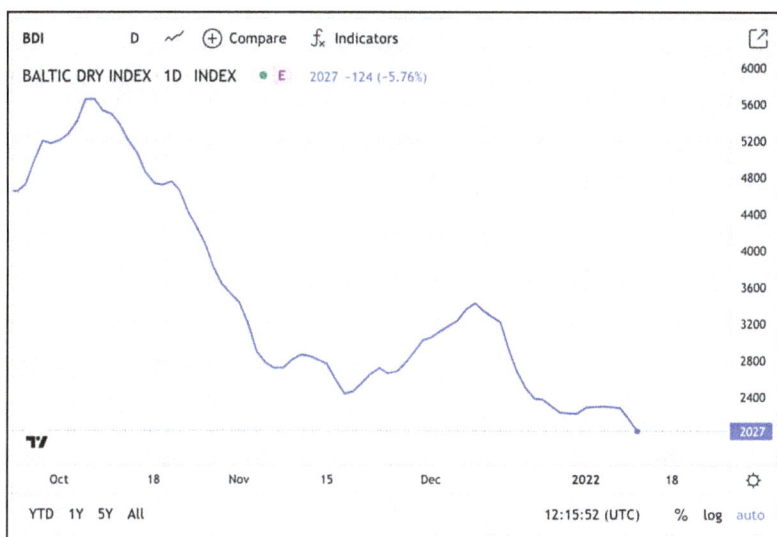

TODAY'S INFLATIONARY PRESSURES ARE LIKE NOTHING WE HAVE EVER SEEN IN AMERICA

All of this leads to more inflation. But contrary to public perception, inflation does not refer to rising prices; they are merely a symptom of inflation. The simple definition is "an increase in the money supply." When money is created out of thin air to provide capital for every stimulus program under the sun—any whim of a politician like infrastructure bills, the Cares Act, Biden's Build Back Better Plan, and so on—all of it adds to the reality that Congress must constantly raise the debt ceiling, pushing us closer to the cliff's edge and a cataclysmic plunge into the abyss. Each new charge on the nation's credit cards more solidifies the impossibility of stopping an inevitable economic overhaul that involves some sort of financial *reset.*

REAL INFLATION IS MUCH HIGHER THAN OFFICIALLY STATED

In their attempt to rein in inflation, the Federal Reserve works at achieving full employment through a system of initiatives that includes:

1. Manipulating interest rates, something we'll talk about later

2. Changing the reserve requirement, which is the percentage of deposited money banks must hold in reserve instead of using for things like lending

3. Increasing or decreasing the money supply as needed

In reality, money supply is never decreased. This is why we experience decades of almost constant inflation, and recent massive increases in money supply have led to this fast-accelerating, upward, inflationary spiral we all see at the cash registers.

As an example to explain the reserve requirement, let's say the Fed sets the requirement at 10% for every $100 deposited into a bank. That means the Fed allows member banks to lend out $90 of each $100, and keep only $10 in available bank capital. Here's the latest craziness about that: As of April 2021, the Fed moved their reserve requirement to *zero*! Technically speaking, this is the Fed acknowledging that their US banking system has become completely starved for capital, so the Fed isn't able to require them to hold *any* capital right now. How quick could a devastating run on a bank be if they can loan out every dollar they have, and even do so many, many times over? Today's banks are not being required to even keep a tiny amount of reserves in case an uncharacteristically large number of people suddenly want their money at the same time. This is a huge problem, and probably a major reason the Fed sent those fifteen banks the "Orderly Resolution Plan."

In an attempt to maintain inflation within a small range or at an explicit target level, the US Government mandates inflation-targeting monetary policy for the Federal Reserve. Having that monumental responsibility, it's crucial for the Fed's means of measuring inflation to be accurate, or policymakers won't be able to effectively control inflation.

This is why I decided to focus my doctoral thesis in an attempt to create a more true gauge of inflation. The dual purpose of my research was to test the accuracy of the current United States inflation estimate that is based on the Consumer Price Index (CPI), and if needed—it was—form a new model for inflation estimation, which I titled the Elliott True Inflation Index (ETII).

THE ETII: ELLIOTT TRUE INFLATION INDEX

$$T = \sum_{i=1}^{10} \beta_i \varpi_i$$

Where:

$i = 1,2,3,\ldots10$

β = Inflation for each subcomponent of GDP as determined by private forecasts

ϖ = Weight of each subcomponent of personal consumption expenditures of GDP. The weight is derived through the following formula: amount of expenditures on a certain item of GDP/Total GDP.

i= The incremental series of each assigned subcomponent of personal | consumption

Source: Elliott, K. (2007). An empirical identification of an appropriate inflation definition and an inflation targeting monetary regime. Ann Arbor, MI: UMI.

To establish the reliability of my new model, I applied quantitative, statistical analysis to examine ever-changing inflation measured by the ETII—versus the CPI that the Fed relies on. The ETII couples external inflation estimates with the actual percentage of consumer spending from Gross Domestic Product (GDP). This method does more accurately arrive at the true rate of inflation by eliminating much of the seasonality, substitution, and other arbitrary bias inherent in the construct of the CPI.

The results of my ETII study show that current inflation estimates, measured by the CPI, are understated compared to real US consumer-consumption patterns. Therefore, policies based on the ETII instead of CPI would have wide-ranging implications. Since inflation forecasts are at the root of so many public-policy issues, a more accurate measurement vehicle for inflation could have an impact globally, giving greater credibility to governments and central banks, something crucial to the longevity of these democratic institutions. The ETII could be used as the measurement vehicle that an inflation-targeting monetary regime is based upon, favorably affecting people's real purchasing power and welfare. Or more simply stated, a better understanding of how much prices are increasing (or decreasing) can be financially life-changing for societies around the world.

Through extensive research, the algorithm I created for ETII is complex, but the resulting method is simple enough for anyone to quickly and accurately gauge the *true* rate of inflation— even calculating it in your head: Multiply Core CPI Inflation by 2.8. The ETII results are in line with what well-known inflation researchers like Dr. John Williams at ShadowStats.com have come up with. But what is the bottom line on US inflation? Well, backing up what you have seen for yourself with how far your hard-earned cash goes these days, according to the unofficial yearly rate of inflation gauged by the ETII, our most recent inflation rate in America is hovering *around 20%*![5, 6, 7]

INCREASING INTEREST RATES

The Federal Reserve has two major tools at its disposal to slow rampant inflation:

1. One way is to stop stimulus (money printing), but considering the present US financial picture, this would kill our economy—so it won't happen. What is Joe Biden's "Brandonomics" plan? [For those who may not know, in the fall of 2021, *Let's Go Brandon* became a popular phrase for *strong* disapproval of Joe Biden and his policies.] Well, at its core his economic policies are delivering two gut punches to American family finances: giving out stimulus and raising taxes. Raising taxes means less money in people's pockets, as stimulus causes the cost of most everything

to rise. Less income and higher prices are an absolute recipe for financial disaster.

2. Because ending stimulus (money printing) is out of the question, the Fed *must* raise interest rates to slow spending as a way to try cutting back on our unrelenting and accelerating price inflation—from all the stimulus. But raising interest rates increases the cost of borrowing for a world saturated with debt (globally, nationally, and individually).

As debt has built up over the decades, policymakers have become more and more reluctant to raise interest rates that can kill economies overnight. A high percentage of people today are living at the margin, completely tapped out. The sad reality is *most* Americans are just one or two missed paychecks away from bankruptcy. If you want continued economic growth, raising borrowing rates for people and governments becomes harder as they get more weighed down by debt. The result is reflected in this chart of long-term interest rates that shows how rates have been steadily pushed down since 1983:

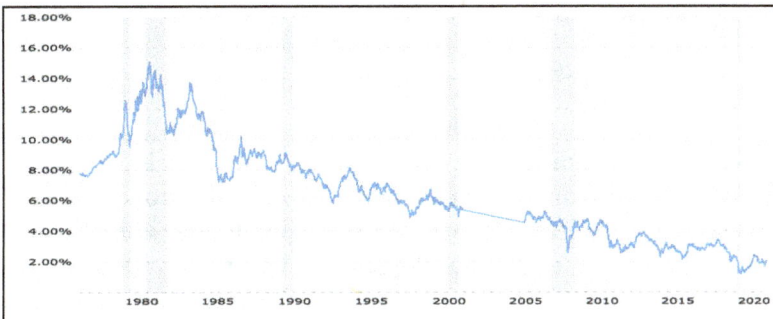

So today, why raise rates that have been inching down for almost four decades, especially when doing so would kill the world's debt-ridden economies? The answer is *inflation*. It has become a worse evil than killing the economy through higher rates. This means Americans living at the margin in 2022 are now faced with horrible tradeoffs, like paying rent versus feeding their families. Today's inflationary pressure has caused imbalances that must be rectified immediately, before we enter a hyperinflationary spiral like current-day Venezuela or the often-cited Weimar Republic (Germany) after WWI.

Either way we go, the result will be catastrophic; thus, we're near the end of an era. What lies immediately ahead for America—and the global economy in which we are enmeshed—will be one for the history books.[8]

HOW DOES IT END?

This chapter started with something we learned as children: lies will always end up being exposed and bring consequences, but those painful repercussions come with a new understanding of the truth, which opens a door to the potential for a more transparent life. There is freedom in that. This same dark-to-light scenario applies to economies around the world that will also fall into chaos when we finally see an end of this ugly central banking era. And it will end. Bottom line—game over.

More than a century of economic revelations will come out about pervasive lying that most all of us believed, to the extreme detriment of our finances. And we will find out how those funds facilitated corrupt people and governments to pull off all sorts of despicable acts. Again, this will bring epic challenges, but the old saying is true:

"It's always darkest before the dawn."

A new day is coming. A new currency is coming. A new era is coming. Through the fast-approaching, non-central-bank "great financial reset," America will emerge much more honorable and prosperous again. But first we pay the piper. Banks will be wiped out. Fortunes will evaporate. People will go to jail as the lies are exposed, but in the end, lessons will be learned—at least for a while—and a sound currency system will rise.

What are you doing in the face of this impending financial disaster? Hopefully you already know what I am going to suggest because many patriots have shut off mainstream media propaganda, instead listening to online truth tellers who have been warning of these problems and recommending the tangible-asset solutions. If you've paid attention to the honest new media, you have probably already begun insulating yourself from the crumbling central bank system. With the right preparation, you and your family need not worry financially.

I suggest tangible assets like gold and silver, a God-given means of exchange, consistently in use for over 5000 years. You can contact my organization to help locate the precious metals you need and even find storage in and out of the US. And be sure to bless others with this book's warnings about the great reset, so your friends, family, and neighbors also have a chance to protect themselves from financial destruction. Contact our team for extensive recommendations on how to protect yourself from America's date with a financial nuclear bomb.

Kirk Elliott PhD Private Advisors can be reached at (720) 605-3900, or visit our website: *KirkElliottPhD.com*. With decades of experience and our belief in people over profits, we can help you navigate the financial Tsunami. Let us walk you through your options, holding your hand and always letting you know when it's time to buy, sell, reallocate, or get out of Dodge. We will do whatever it takes to protect and preserve all you have worked to accumulate.

CHAPTER 3

WHY PRECIOUS METALS NOW?

There is a right time for every ethical investment: sometimes stocks make sense, other times bonds, real estate has its up moves, and often precious metals are the biggest winners. With this chapter I will lay out the reasons gold and silver make sense for everyone's portfolio today. Your financial success—and the safety of your savings—critically depends on understanding the economic situation we are living through right now.

America is a constitutional-republic form of government that the 18th-century Scottish professor Alexander Fraser Tytler included in his look at the major problem with *democratic-type* governments:

"A democracy cannot exist as a permanent form of government. It can only exist until the voters discover that they can vote themselves [more and more money] from the public treasury."

At some point the citizens will have voted to take so much from the treasury that the nation becomes broke. He goes on:

"From that moment on, the majority always votes for the candidates promising the most benefits from the public treasury with the result that a democracy always collapses over loose fiscal policy, always followed by a dictatorship."

The average our world's greatest civilizations have lasted has been around 200years. Since the United States became a nation in 1776, we are 246 years into what Tytler called the cycle of democracy, something he explains this way:

"These nations have progressed through this sequence: From bondage to spiritual faith; From spiritual faith to great courage; From courage to liberty; From liberty to abundance; From abundance to selfishness; From selfishness to apathy; From apathy to dependence; From dependence back into bondage."[9]

Where is the United States in this cycle? We appear to be in the apathy stage, headed toward dependence and bondage. With our apathetic America today, we see the vast majority distracted by work and entertainment to the point that they have stopped caring to research the important issues of our time—just trusting a completely untrustworthy government.

Has the US been following Tytler's cycle? Yes. Our ancestors were in bondage to England but wanted religious liberty, so they left Europe to find a new land where they could have that freedom. They mostly achieved it in America, though England continued controlling us as much as they could. Our taste of liberty gave us great courage to fight the Revolutionary War for a chance at total independence. We won, and when able to direct our own destiny, we saw our liberty lead to abundance.

Hard work brought widespread wealth and a strong future for families. From there the contentedness of fat wallets (keeping the full reward of our hard work) caused us to fall into selfishness: when allowed, many people tend toward taking. Self-focus led to overspending, which has caused our nation to be massively indebted. Widespread self-serving has made much of our society complacent. Fat and happy people get lazy and stop caring; they just want what they want. Now at the apathy stage, most Americans have been neglecting even the simplest checks on government power, like keeping a skeptical eye on voter fraud. And many won't even take an hour to vote every once in a while. This disregard is leading to more and more dependence on the decisions of corrupt leadership, who have driven us to an imminent bankruptcy—where they gain total control and throw us back into bondage.

America's current apathy stage is where nations lose their soul: a despondent society demands that government take care of them with free food and healthcare, subsidized housing, extra cash even before retirement, and then a steady check after they're done working. Whether they deserve the benefits or not, many citizens vote out politicians not willing to hand out free stuff, always looking for those who will be more accommodating.

Later I will go into more detail on this, but America is now way past any sort of financial sanity. Social Security, Medicare, Medicaid, and accompanying mandatory programs (like food stamps and others aimed at helping women, infants, and children) are costing us $4.02 trillion. Yet our government will collect only $4.17 trillion during all of 2022. So total entitlements like those above take 96% of all federal revenue, and interest on the national debt this year will add $305 billion to the bill. That brings US spending to 103% of revenues, putting us over budget, so that deficit gets added to our already-insurmountable, US national debt of $30.5 trillion.

Proposed Budget by Category
(In billions of dollars)

	2020	2021	2022	2023	2024	2025	2026	2027	2028	2029	2030	2031	2022-2026	2022-2031
Outlays:														
Discretionary programs:														
Defense	714	735	756	756	775	791	804	816	826	835	843	851	3,881	8,052
Non-defense	913	960	932	930	909	914	917	927	947	964	984	1,002	4,601	9,426
Subtotal, discretionary programs	1,627	1,696	1,688	1,685	1,683	1,704	1,721	1,743	1,773	1,799	1,827	1,854	8,482	17,478
Mandatory programs:														
Social Security	1,090	1,135	1,196	1,261	1,333	1,410	1,492	1,579	1,672	1,767	1,866	1,966	6,691	16,542
Medicare	769	706	766	841	TOTAL SOCIAL SECURITY, MEDICARE, MEDICAID, and									3
Medicaid	458	621	571	585	MANDATORY PAYMENTS: $4.02T +$305B interest=$4.32T									6
Other mandatory programs	2,280	2,889	1,486	1,322										1
Subtotal, mandatory programs	4,578	5,351	4,018	4,008	4,196	4,388	4,501	4,589	4,685	4,882	5,191	5,444	21,021	46,960
Net interest	345	303	305	320	368	445	524	603	674	744	829	914	1,962	5,726
Total outlays	6,550	7,349	6,011	6,013	6,187	6,508	6,746	6,935	7,312	7,425	7,847	8,211	31,465	69,196
Receipts:														
Individual income taxes	1,609	1,705	2,039	2,242	2,288	2,436	2,676	2,896	3,044	3,194	3,354	3,526	11,680	27,694
Corporation income taxes	212	268	371	577	649	673	664	666	679	676	681	693	2,933	6,330
Social insurance and retirement receipts:														
Social Security payroll taxes	965	944	1,033	1,072	1,118	1,159	1,207	1,252	1,311	1,361	1,417	1,474	5,587	12,403
Medicare payroll taxes	292	287	359	383	400	418	436	453	476	496	518	540	1,996	4,478
Unemployment insurance	43	55	59	61	60	57	55	55	57	56	56	56	293	576
Other retirement	10	10	11	12	12	13	13	14	15	16	17	17	62	140
Excise taxes	87	74	84	89	93	94	95	96	96	96	101	102	455	948
Estate and gift taxes	18	18	21	18	TOTAL FEDERAL REVENUE $4.17T									4
Customs duties	69	85	57	46	ENTITLEMENTS + MANDATORY PAYMENTS = 96% of FED									6
Deposits of earnings, Federal Reserve System	102	97	109	100	REVENUE									4
Other miscellaneous receipts	36	37	39	41										1
Total receipts	3,421	3,581	4,174	4,641										5
Deficit	3,129	3,869	1,837	1,372	ADD INTEREST ON OUR NATIONAL DEBT + ENTITLEMENTS									1
Net interest	345	303	305	320	AND MANDATORY PAYMENTS = 103% of FED REVENUE									6
Primary deficit	2,784	3,366	1,532	1,052										6
On-budget deficit	3,142	3,696	1,789	1,301	1,284	1,341	1,260	1,115	1,205	1,045	1,174	1,223	6,936	12,718
Off-budget deficit/surplus (−)	−13	73	48	71	95	129	154	189	219	262	303	345	496	1,813

Sounds like a challenging situation, but prepare to hear about our financial doom: none of that includes what we will spend in 2022 on yearly, necessary costs like infrastructure, government, education, and defense. Adding those will bring US spending to about $6 trillion for 2022—when government will only bring in a bit over $4 trillion! How long would your family last doing that each year? Of course you and I have no printing press like the federal government does, so they will just devalue our currency more by overproducing US dollars. This will continue to push inflation higher, further ramping up the robbing of Americans' purchasing power, at least until the day our nation's money becomes worthless.

All this means it is impossible for the US to balance the federal budget unless entitlements are *severely* slashed. But politicians will not do that because cutting entitlements means losing votes. So they will print and print, and in that way steal more and more money from Americans who the government schools—purposely—never educate on the cause of inflation, money printing. This leaves us with less money in our pockets, purses, and savings and an already out-of-control financial situation with a looming entitlement time bomb that worsens each year.

One reason entitlement spending will only get worse is the US fertility rate. In fact, one of the scariest trends in world history is the fertility rate of industrialized nations today. I go in depth into this in chapter 8, but briefly, the US and most other economically powerful countries around the world are at fertility rates below two, meaning when two adults die, they (on average) are not replacing themselves with at least two children. This causes the economic output of a nation to shrink as the population ages, with more people entering retirement years and receiving benefits, compared to those left working and paying into the system.

When originally set up, those entitlements that politicians gave us were established as Ponzi schemes: our leaders knew the entire system would eventually collapse when too few were paying in for all those collecting benefits. But when nations go into financial chaos, governments are able to take more control, so the uppermost tier of powerful people often fosters economic tragedy for the little guy, in hopes of taking more of their money while grabbing greater control with *a reset.* And politicians want votes, so few are interested in cutting entitlements; thus, the problem does not get solved until an economy crashes. Here is where the world's most affluent nations are right now with fertility rates:

- France: 2.0
- United Kingdom: 2.0
- United States: 1.9
- Norway: 1.9
- Australia: 1.9
- Sweden: 1.9
- Brazil: 1.8
- Iran: 1.6

- Canada: 1.6
- China: 1.6
- Russia: 1.5
- Switzerland: 1.5
- Japan: 1.4
- Germany: 1.4
- Italy: 1.4
- Singapore: 1.2

Source: worldbank.org

These most economically powerful nations of the world are all below a sustainable growth rate. Even if policies were enacted immediately to entice people to have more children—like rewarding families who have five kids with not having to pay taxes—a nation could not fix their problem until that flood of babies start reaching full-time work at adulthood. And even if we could last that long financially, is this sort of policy change likely to be enacted? Possibly by only a few nations, like Russia, whose new policy was mentioned in an August 2022 article. Russia is now "offering a hero's medal and $16,000 to women who have 10 kids."[10]

Either way the global economy certainly does not have that much time before the entitlement time bombs explode, causing an unprecedented number of hyperinflationary recessions all around the world. And each country that crashes harms the rest, accelerating the dominoes falling. Hoping to avoid the death of their money, nations have already been massively inflating their currencies for years. But that is why their money will die. There is no other outcome. They need a reset. They are trapped. It's almost over.

Most nations today are facing the end of the central-bankers Ponzi scheme, a system given to them many decades ago by a private banking cartel (the beneficiaries of inflation) that has robbed all those sovereign nations of their ability to print their own currency. The bankers are the ones who benefit from currency creation, as they print and loan the money to us at interest, rather than our nation printing our own money and paying zero interest on any of it.

And the ugly side of politics is that our politicians will just keep spending to keep themselves in office. Then as they run out of money, they will begin taking crazier and crazier steps, like *increased* spending meant to stimulate economic growth. They even create more public-sector jobs to get more people spending, but those jobs take money out of taxpayer pockets. So public-sector employees might spend more, but it is offset by private-sector workers having less to spend. Public policy often does nothing or even destroys revenue, making the situation worse. This problem was first written on a dinner napkin by University of Chicago professor Arthur Laffer, who was enlightening Donald Rumsfeld and Dick Cheney when they were discussing President Gerald Ford's plan to curtail inflation:[11]

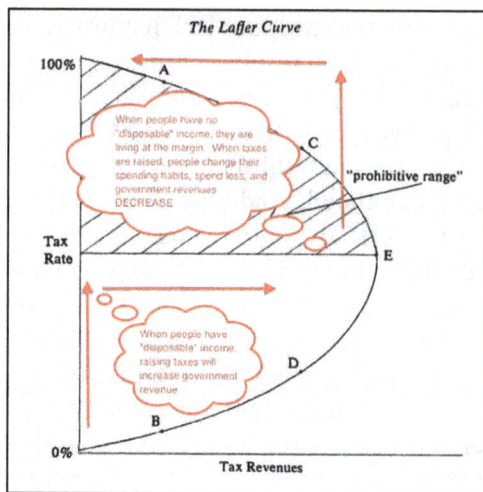

The Laffer Curve

The Laffer Curve shows how much revenue various tax rates can be expected to bring in for government. The takeaway is that financially fat and happy people who have money left over at the end of the month are not as impacted by taxes going up, so they have enough money that they are likely to keep spending a similar amount. This allows the government to tax that person more *and* expect them to continue spending the same amount, something that also brings in government revenue.

But Laffer warned that there is always a point where more taxes actually begin causing a diminishing return for governments. That happens when people run out of disposable (extra) income, which means they had been living at their spending limits, so the added taxes cause them to decrease spending—decreasing government revenue. The taxes bring in more but cause financially stretched people to spend less, so government revenue can begin going down at that point, even though taxes were raised again.

In America today, that tax-increase issue is a major problem because the vast majority of us are living at the margin, while Washington, DC politicians are still looking to raise taxes as they run out of money. And whatever they can't tax from the people, they just print out of thin air, causing increased inflation that takes more money from hard-working Americans. With those sorts of detrimental actions, consumer spending takes a dive as inflation rises, lowering government revenues that much more. And we are already spending 50% more than what we bring in, so any increased taxes now will decrease US revenues, because we are already far into Laffer's prohibitive range.

Rather than that recipe for failure—where government continues bankrupting the nation by *increasing* taxes and the money supply (causing inflation)—a successful direction change would come from stimulating the economy by *decreasing* government spending and *lowering* taxes.

Now let's look at interest rates. Bond *yield* is the *interest rate* people earn from buying bonds. Interest rates move opposite bond prices (bonds going up equal rates coming down and vice versa). When bonds are losing value, those holding them have to be enticed to stay with the bonds by giving them greater yield on their bond investment. Besides bonds going up with decreased yield, this chart t shows how stocks will also move up with decreasing interest rates (yield):

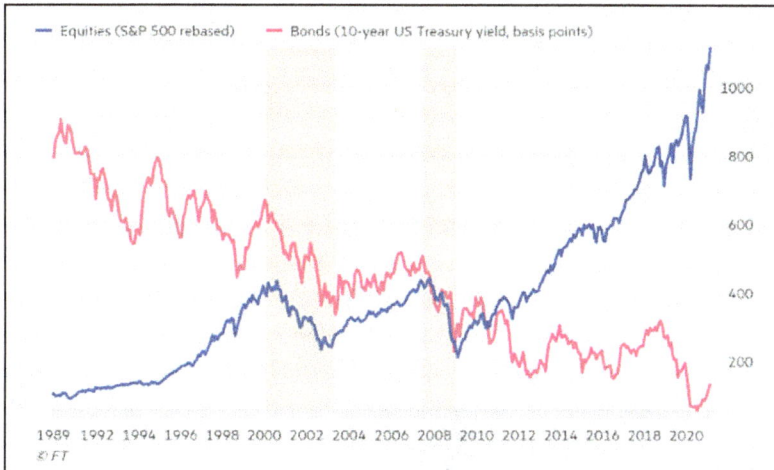

Decreasing interest rates stimulate more and more spending, which increases business revenues and profits—so stocks go up. Lower interest makes borrowing increasingly affordable, causing people to borrow and spend more. In fact, Americans have been the biggest spenders on the planet for a long time, leaving us a sad legacy of passing insurmountable debt to future generations. But it will not get that far: the overspending has been so excessive that our nation faces the economy blowing up any day now, rather than making our financially shackled children cover $30 trillion (and rising rapidly). Over the past two years alone, we irresponsible adults have printed more currency than our ancestors did in the first 244 years.[12]

The opposite scenario adds another problem when interest rates (bond yields) inevitably go back up: stocks and bonds move down—as seen in 2022. Throughout history we have seen that long-term changes in the direction of interest rates have happened on average every 28 years. Here are interest rates going back to 1800:

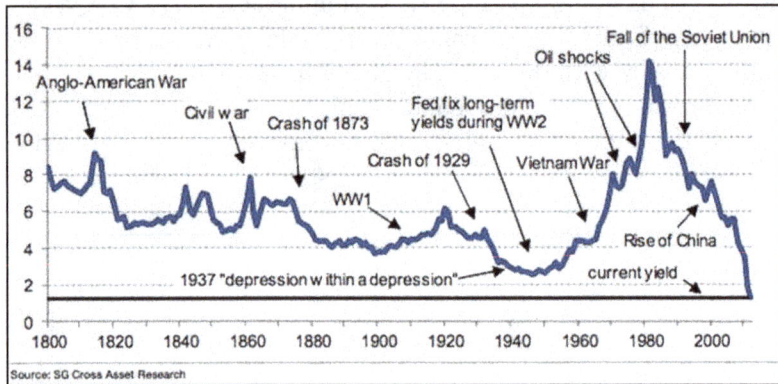

The US piled up over $30 trillion in debt, as our government has lowered interest rates since 1983, and then kept them at extreme artificial lows for most of the past twenty years. Some reading this may remember the 1980s when buying a home on a 30-year mortgage meant paying 18% interest—those are modern credit card rates! No one these days would pay that on a mortgage, but it was common back then. During the past couple decades, we have seen a few times when government hiked interest rates off the extreme lows, only to reverse course and abandon those efforts after dampened consumer spending that began wiping out the economy. Their actions were intended to slow the inflation they created by printing more and more money out of thin air, but terrible economies do not help politicians get reelected.

In 2022 interest rates have had nowhere to go but up, which has meant stocks and bonds coming down—a reliable inverse correlation. When interest rates rise, bond markets get absolutely crushed, and that is true whether the bonds are federal, municipal, corporate, or any others. As this chart shows, over long-term periods since the 1940s, stocks and bonds have typically moved in the opposite direction from interest rates (the Federal Funds Rate):

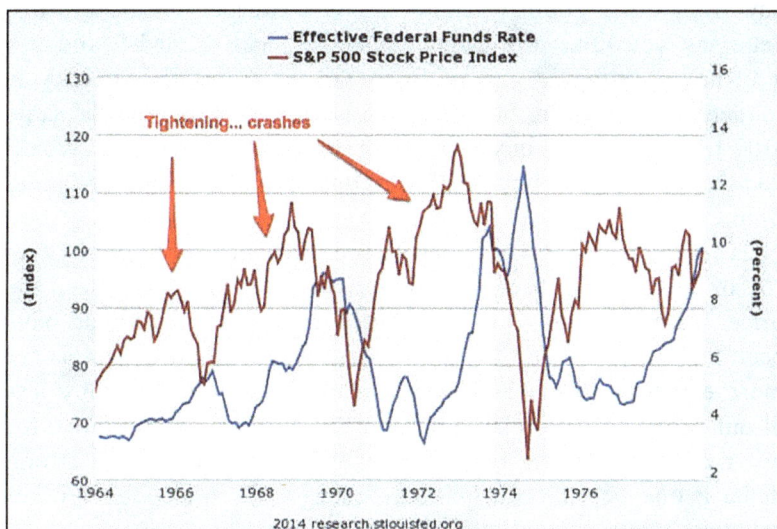

On top of that, imagine that the US has many states where *no one* works, meaning all those people are riding in the societal wagon, taking money from the government. For whatever justified or unjustified reasons, none of those Americans are helping pull the wagon, working and paying taxes to increase government revenues. I go into more detail later, but quickly, the US has some ugly employment math today: 12.38 million Americans are on disability and 11.62 million more are unemployed, for a total of 24 million not working, which equals the combined population of Wyoming, Vermont, the District of Columbia, North Dakota, South Dakota, Alaska, Delaware, Montana, Rhode Island, New Hampshire, Maine, Hawaii, Idaho, West Virginia, Nebraska, New Mexico, Nevada, Mississippi, and Kansas.

The total number of Americans not in the labor force is approaching 100 million, almost a third of our population—historically high numbers. Why is that? We have an aging, retiring population and a working-age public with 24 million unemployed. These are serious problems. We are in trouble! This can't last.

Those issues can be protected against by owning precious metals. What else points to purchasing gold and silver right now?

America has had a strong dollar since the Clinton administration, which means foreign countries (with less valuable currency) need to pay more for American goods. And imported products we buy from other countries have become cheaper for Americans. Let's say you cross the Canadian border with $100 US and use it to buy a shopping cart of food. Then if Canada's currency is suddenly devalued by 50% (relative to the US dollar), your same $100 US would now buy two shopping carts full of food. Would you be inclined to buy groceries domestically or import them from Canada?

Today the strong US dollar has resulted in Americans buying 70% of what we consume from other countries. This has caused the prices we pay for goods to be *deflated* from what they would have been had we continued buying American. But when US goods are more expensive overseas, foreigners and their countries buy less of our products. The relatively high US dollar creates *inflation* for other nations wanting to purchase American goods. So a strong dollar is one way to boost manufacturing and service jobs in other countries while causing more American unemployment.

As we purchase more and more foreign goods, we export American jobs to other countries who produce what we buy. Americans love to spend—we are a consumerist economy—and we want to pay less, so we buy cheap stuff from other nations, which has meant exporting jobs. Would you buy your daughter a Barbie doll for $30 from a US manufacturer, or pay $15 from companies like Costco, Amazon, or Walmart who sell a lot of China-manufactured products? The vast majority of Americans would purchase the $15 doll.

In order to have more jobs in America, we need to get the rest of the world to buy our stuff. How? Through a weak-dollar policy that encourages imports, which makes foreign goods and services more expensive and our exports more affordable for other nations. Because of American ingenuity—and the US culture they have been seeing for many decades through our television and movies—people in other nations often prefer buying our products and services. We just need to help them afford what we make and do. Again, it takes less foreign currency to buy American products when we have a weak US dollar, so we bring back American jobs by supporting that goal; the right economic policy understands that people around the globe want cheap goods and services. Often working against that objective are American wholesalers and retailers who rely heavily on imports. They do better with a higher US dollar that buys more from other countries.

A weakening US dollar inversely correlates with rising interest rates and inflation. A weakened American currency would come from fewer people around the planet wanting to invest in our nation's central-bank money, what we call Federal Reserve Notes or US Treasuries. Every US dollar is a loan from the private central bankers who print them, adding to the American debt—that we pay interest on. Foreigners and their nations are more enticed to invest in our "debt" (US Treasuries, or US currency) as we increase the interest rate we are willing to pay them.

But a weaker US dollar would mean the prices Americans pay for imported goods would go up—that's inflation—because Americans would still buy those products for a while: it always takes time for consumer behavior to shift. So even if we do the right thing by weakening the US dollar (to bring back jobs), that too would mean more inflation.

So how can policymakers slow inflation? First, they must raise interest rates to slow borrowing by Americans and US companies. This rate increase will then cause both to spend less because they are more handcuffed by increased interest payments on their current debt. Less spending hurts businesses, so they lay off workers and their stock value goes down.

Another way to slow inflation is to quit printing so much US currency. But politicians will not do that when stimulus money may be their only action to keep the economy afloat and get reelected. Instead, they keep kicking the can down the road for the next Congress to fix—who won't quit printing either because no policymaker wants to kill the economy. And because we as a nation and most individuals are shackled with debt, there is zero will to raise interest rates to historically normal levels. Again, that would hamper spending, bringing down the stock market.

An opposite approach to tackle inflation is to simply let the stock and bond markets collapse, exactly where our current economic policies seem to be taking us. When markets fall, people lose jobs, they spend less, and that brings down corporate revenues. This results in more layoffs, so even less money is spent, which worsens the corporate revenue problem. Conversely, when more people are working, spending rises, which increases corporate revenues. This causes companies to hire more, and a working society spends more, further increasing corporate hiring. Without nations taking drastic actions to turn around a sick global economy, we cannot hope to right economic troubles.

We talked about the Baltic Dry Index (BDI) in the last chapter, but I want to repeat a few aspects and give you a bit more detail in the next couple paragraphs: the BDI is a worldwide indicator of global economic health and serves as a warning sign for economic trouble. Today the BDI is sounding a dire alarm about a planetary economic slowdown of cataclysmic proportions. Again, the BDI measures the world's demand for manufacturing ingredients like coal, steel, cement, and iron ore. The lack of demand for these raw materials becomes apparent when fewer of the huge cargo ships are seen traveling the world's waterways. When more product is being sold and delivered around the planet, the index performs well, reflecting significant manufacturing in nations like China, Indonesia, and Australia; they are buying a lot of materials to build things. When the index is down, demand for raw materials has slumped because international commerce has slowed. Here is how the BDI has looked for over ten years:

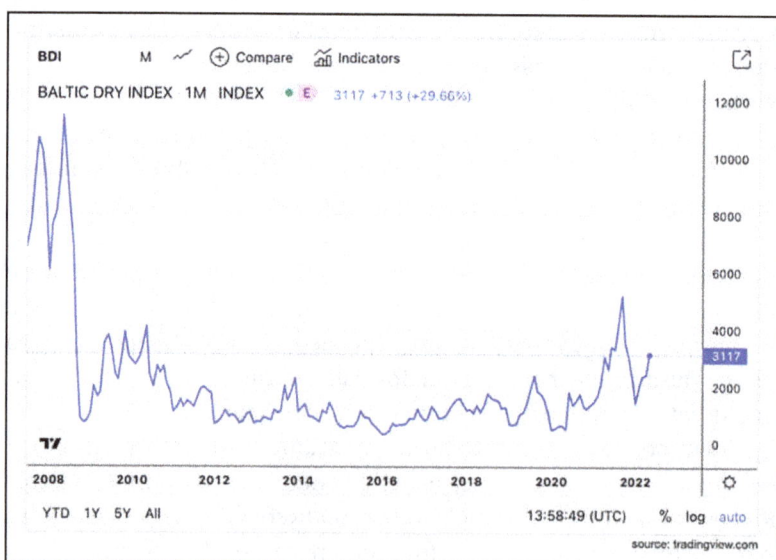

For over a decade the Baltic Dry Index has shown low activity levels for ships on the water, down 89% since its peak in May 2008.

We have been in the midst of an unprecedented and lengthy global economic slowdown. So, summarizing the US situation that is shared by much of the world, we are *loaded with debt*, interest rates are rising, inflation is raging, and politicians are working diligently to increase our taxes—all this as the world is being ravaged by a massive economic slowdown. Even with all that, there is at least one investment that will safeguard your savings through the current financial catastrophe facing America and most of the world. Of course I am talking about precious metals.

As mentioned earlier, besides unethical investments, there are no awful places to put your money, only terrible timing. What are the implications of the pendulum swing to rising interest rates, especially right now? The US and much of the world are in debt up to their eyeballs, including at the national, state, municipal, and individual levels. Most Americans and our global neighbors are living paycheck to paycheck at the margins, which means just a couple paychecks away from filing bankruptcy. Now imagine hiked interest rates that greatly increase all that debt! It means most every government and person gets squeezed, while they have no capacity to withstand the ramped-up interest payments. When families have no money left at the end of the month, what happens if their debt increases and income does not? They decrease spending, sell stuff, or dip into investments and savings—the rainy day has arrived!

What are the economic results of these family cutbacks? Corporate America becomes less profitable, stocks go down, and people get laid off, so folks spend less and that further hurts businesses. For governments, fewer citizens working mean lower revenue from sales and income taxes, causing deeply indebted, cash-starved governments to consider drastic measures. These include big-business bailouts that cause more inflation because bailouts mean massive money printing. Those in control may also instigate bail-*ins* for failing banks, which means family checking and savings accounts suddenly get frozen, after which the banksters confiscate some of that money, rescuing themselves from bankruptcy. Financially strapped governments become more and more imaginative with those and other austerity measures that rob the people—at times when families are already financially suffering at the margin.

So right now, around the world, bailouts, bail-ins, and other austerity measures have been used, and more are coming. And as I just mentioned, inflation is hitting in a huge way, interest rates are rising quickly from all-time lows, and global, national, corporate, state, municipal, and personal debt are at all-time highs. This financial turmoil is happening as the vast majority of Americans and others are living paycheck to paycheck, not able to withstand any sort of financially worsening situation, like the one bearing down on them now—the day of reckoning is near!

All that said, and keeping in mind what I mentioned about appropriate timing for every investment, let's look at what is happening today with the market cycles of four prominently held investments. Bonds are getting crushed as interest rates rise. The stock market is down 15% from its high and looks to be headed much lower as we slip into a recession. Real estate is topping out and turning down because people do not pay cash for houses; instead, they finance them, meaning fewer and fewer people can afford housing as their cost of borrowing (interest rates) quickly goes up. Right now every policy coming out of Washington, DC is negative for stocks, bonds, and real estate.

So what do we do? Well, the exact fundamentals that cause those three major asset classes to come *down* also drive the price of gold and silver *up*. Increasing debt and interest rates, high inflation, political chaos from government policies, and geo-political conflict all cause stocks, bonds, mutual funds, and real estate to come down. But those sorts of economic issues boost the price of gold and silver.

With investment timing often dependent on whether government is growth-minded or taking actions that shrink the economy, everything we have talked about so far points to higher gold and silver prices. And that trend will accelerate as people in financial turmoil all over the world turn more and more to the safety of metals. How do you protect yourself during times of inflation? You invest in tangible assets that go up with inflation. Tesla and SpaceX billionaire Elon Musk is worth a quarter of a trillion dollars. When he was asked how he protects his finances from inflation, Musk said the answer is easy: buy things that go up with inflation, like cars, steel, oil, and natural gas.

Though we do not have his resources—or bills—we've all seen the huge increase in grocery prices. Suddenly feeding families has become challenging, even for many in the middle-class. So what are some tangible assets we can easily own and transport? Silver and gold. If you want to inoculate yourself against inflation and other consequences of the globalist politicians (like vast numbers of jobs being exported out of America), buy gold and silver for such a time as this. Protect your savings!

Over the centuries, precious metals have *by far* been the world's safest asset. And for the foreseeable future, they are set to also provide the highest growth of any investment. In today's asset-decimating environment, precious metals offer savings safety *and growth*. Of course you always want to minimize risk while maximizing returns. At this time in the cycles of various major investments, you must move out of those that are drifting lower and even plunging, and shift a significant percentage of your life savings into gold and silver—as soon as possible.

To discuss your own situation, call us at Kirk Elliott PhD Private Advisors (720-605-3900) or visit our website at *KirkElliottPhD.com*. Let us walk you through your options. We believe in people over profits. Our company has the decades of experience needed to help you navigate through this storm, holding your hand and always letting you know when it's time to buy, sell, reallocate, get out of Dodge, or do whatever it takes to protect and preserve everything you've worked to accumulate.

Because your retirement and assets are important to you, they are important to us. How do you deal with the insane policies of today's politicians? Buy gold and silver. We can help. Call us.

CHAPTER 4

A COMPARATIVE ANALYSIS OF RETURNS ON INFLATION-ADJUSTED INVESTMENTS FROM 2000 TO 2022

Inflation is crucially important to every American, and the level of *official* inflation claimed by the government's CPI has extremely understated real, actual inflation that I call *unofficial*. *Official* inflation is understated—your wallet tells you that. What is the accurate, *unofficial* rate of inflation? As mentioned in a previous chapter, during my doctoral dissertation I developed a new methodology for measuring inflation, which I call the ETII (Elliott True Inflation Index). It more accurately represents the true inflation rate by nationally identifying the actual price of goods that consumers are paying and then applying the proper weighting as identified by US Gross Domestic Product (GDP).

I want to give you a bit more detail on the ETII: with a possible 25% margin of error (that can only err on the side of understating the problem), the ETII tells us that official inflation has been *understated* by 285.33%. According to the US government's Consumer Price Index, or CPI (their gauge of current "official" inflation), for May of 2022 alone, inflation was 8.3%. But based on my research—which correlates well with well-known and respected researcher John Williams of *ShadowStats.com*—the true (unofficial) inflation for May 2022 was between 23.68% and 29.60%. And average annual inflation since the year 2000 has been 7.16%.

Now with inflation in mind, let's look at some common investments that all of us may have made, analyzing how each has performed since the year 2000:

REAL RETURN ON CDs

The current interest rate earned on a one-year CD (Certificate of Deposit) is 1%, and most people believe CDs guarantee they will not lose money. But with the true rate of unofficial inflation averaging 7.16% annually, the real guarantee of a CD since the year 2000 has meant you were guaranteed to *lose* 121% of your investment. Your purchasing power has been *losing* an average of 5.52% per year. So since 2000, CDs have had a total gain of 36.02% (1.64% per year), but when you account for inflation, you *lost* an average of 5.52% each year—a guaranteed horrible outcome![13, 14]

REAL RETURN ON TREASURY BONDS

Since 2000 the total return on a thirty-year Treasury bond has been 63.99% (2.91% per year). With inflation at 7.16% on average, this investment *lost* an average of 4.25% purchasing power per year.[15, 16]

REAL RETURN ON STOCKS

In 2000, the Dow Jones Industrial Average was 11,239. Almost twenty-two years later, the DJIA is near all-time highs at 36,338. Some years have been up and others down, but even though the market has come down to almost 30,000 as I write this, we will go with the high figure over 36,000, which reflects an average annual growth rate of 7.57%. With inflation at 7.16% per year on average, a broad-based stock portfolio would have grown your buying power at a rate of less than half of 1% (0.41% per year).[17]

REAL RETURN ON REAL ESTATE

In 2000, the median US home price was $185,800, and it is currently $453,700, up 144.18% since 2000 (averaging 4.77% per year). But accounting for 7.16% inflation each year, real estate is down 2.39% per year.[18]

REAL RETURN ON GOLD AND SILVER

In 2000, gold was $289 per ounce and is now $1829 at the time of writing this, for a total increase of 532.87% (an average increase of 9.86% per year). Deducting inflation, gold is still up on average of 2.7% each year. In 2000, silver started the year at $5.10 per ounce and is now $24.54. That is up 381.1% since 2000 (a 10.09% gain per year). Taking inflation out, silver is still up on average of 2.93% each year.[19, 20]

FOR THIS CENTURY SO FAR—LIKE EVERY PREVIOUS ONE—WHAT HAS BEEN THE BEST INVESTMENT TO PROTECT AND PRESERVE YOUR SAVINGS?

It is gold and silver! The only way to safeguard your savings is to outpace the true, unofficial inflation. In this study, I went all the way back to 2000 so we would be looking at *long-term* analysis. Asset classes go up and down at different times, but two decades is long enough for each to experience ups and downs. Here are the results:

CDs:	−5.52% per year
Bonds:	−4.25% per year
Real Estate:	−2.39% per year
Stocks:	+0.41% per year
Gold:	+2.70% per year
Silver:	+2.93% per year

Though the stock market has come down since I did this study near its peak, I was shocked to learn that stocks were not the best performer. As you can see, for protection and preservation over the past two decades, the only three assets that posted positive returns when adjusted for inflation were gold, silver, and maybe stocks if they haven't fallen too much since this study. Here's a chart of my analysis and then a detailed look at the data:

YEAR	ASSET CLASS						INFLATION MEASUREMENTS		
	30 yr Bond	CD	GOLD	SILVER	DJIA	REAL ESTATE	CPI	ETI (TRUE INFLATION)	Upper Range
2000	6.63%	5.01%	$ 289 1.00%	$ 5.10 -0.58%	11,239.98 20.17%	$ 165,300 5.02%	3.40%	9.70%	12.13%
2001	5.54%	5.33%	$ 268 -7.18%	$ 4.52 -11.37%	10,659.26 -5.17%	$ 169,800 2.72%	2.80%	7.99%	9.99%
2002	5.45%	2.14%	$ 278 3.77%	$ 4.72 4.42%	9,876.68 -7.34%	$ 188,700 11.13%	1.60%	4.57%	5.71%
2003		1.47%	$ 347 24.94%	$ 4.84 2.54%	8,389.13 -15.06%	$ 186,000 -1.43%	2.30%	6.56%	8.20%
2004		1.15%	$ 422 21.66%	$ 6.22 28.51%	10,528.94 25.51%	$ 212,700 14.35%	2.70%	7.70%	9.63%
2005		2.08%	$ 436 3.13%	$ 6.47 4.02%	10,539.66 0.10%	$ 232,500 9.31%	3.40%	9.70%	12.13%
2006		3.28%	$ 513 17.77%	$ 8.95 38.33%	10,857.48 3.02%	$ 247,700 6.54%	3.20%	9.13%	11.41%
2007	4.85%	3.78%	$ 632 23.20%	$ 12.88 43.91%	12,565.33 15.73%	$ 257,400 3.92%	2.80%	7.99%	9.99%
2008	4.33%	3.51%	$ 833 31.80%	$ 14.80 14.91%	12,413.99 -1.20%	$ 233,900 -9.13%	3.80%	10.84%	13.55%
2009	3.13%	1.79%	$ 870 4.41%	$ 10.97 -25.88%	8,239.70 -33.63%	$ 208,400 -10.90%	-0.40%	-1.14%	-1.43%
2010	4.60%	0.81%	$ 1,088 25.04%	$ 18.64 69.92%	10,296.09 24.96%	$ 222,900 6.96%	1.60%	4.57%	5.71%
2011	4.52%	0.48%	$ 1,406 29.24%	$ 28.31 51.88%	12,241.21 18.89%	$ 226,900 1.79%	3.20%	9.13%	11.41%
2012	3.03%	0.34%	$ 1,598 13.70%	$ 33.72 19.11%	12,605.03 2.97%	$ 238,400 5.07%	2.10%	5.99%	7.49%
2013	3.08%	0.28%	$ 1,658 3.72%	$ 31.11 -7.74%	13,760.98 9.17%	$ 258,400 8.39%	1.50%	4.28%	5.35%
2014	3.77%	0.23%	$ 1,205 -27.33%	$ 20.39 -34.46%	16,118.39 17.13%	$ 275,200 6.50%	1.60%	4.57%	5.71%
2015	2.46%	0.27%	$ 1,206 0.12%	$ 16.54 -18.88%	17,521.62 8.71%	$ 296,500 7.74%	0.10%	0.29%	0.36%
2016	2.86%	0.27%	$ 1,060 -12.11%	$ 13.86 -16.20%	16,219.86 -7.43%	$ 312,800 5.50%	1.30%	3.71%	4.64%
2017	3.02%	0.36%	$ 1,229 15.94%	$ 16.22 17.03%	22,000.00 35.64%	$ 313,100 0.10%	1.60%	4.57%	5.71%
2018	3.10%	0.33%	$ 1,281 4.23%	$ 15.46 -4.69%	23,062.40 4.83%	$ 362,400 4.00%	1.90%	5.42%	6.78%
2019	2.39%	0.51%	$ 1,520 18.60%	$ 17.78 15.00%	28,462.00 23.41%	$ 312,500 -13.76%	1.80%	5.14%	6.42%
2020	1.56%	1.60%	$ 1,894 24.60%	$ 26.30 47.90%	30,606.48 7.50%	$ 391,900 25.40%	5.40%	15.41%	19.26%
2021	2.06%	1.00%	$ 1,829 -3.40%	$ 24.54 10.70%	36,338.30 18.70%	$ 453,700 15.80%	7.50%	21.40%	26.75%
Sum	63.99%	36.02%	216.86%	211.98%	166.60%	105.01%	55.20%	157.50%	196.85%
Annual Average	2.91%	1.64%	9.86%	10.09%	7.57%	4.77%	2.51%	7.16%	8.95%
Inflation Adjusted Return	-4.25%	-5.52%	2.70%	2.93%	0.41%	-2.39%			

RESEARCH SUMMARY			
	% OF TIME RETURN > INFLATION	ANNUAL AVERAGE	ANNUALIZED AFTER INFLATION
BONDS	17%	2.91%	-4.25%
GOLD	55%	9.86%	2.7%
SILVER	45%	10.09%	2.93%
STOCKS	56%	7.57%	0.41%
CD	5%	1.64%	-5.52%
REAL ESTATE	50%	4.77%	-2.39%

As these trends continue and even accelerate with the deteriorating US debt and inflation situation—like most larger nations around the world—expect to see much higher prices in tangible assets like gold and silver, and more losses in stocks, bonds, real estate, and CDs. This trend should continue until a significant change in market fundamentals, signaling a major shift.

When we are able to sift through all the disinformation, the choice is easy; that is, *if* we can deprogram ourselves from a lifetime of wrongly believing that certain investments are the safe ones. There are few terrible investments—just favorable or unfavorable timing.

CHAPTER 5

FROM THE TURN OF THE CENTURY, WHAT HAS BEEN THE BEST INVESTMENT?

The following is taken from an article in the December 2020 edition of Don S. McAlvany's monthly *McAlvany Intelligence Advisor* (*MIA*) newsletter. I have greatly paraphrased the article for simplicity, consistency, and flow with the rest of this book:

Since the 1970s, our researchers at the MIA have been actively engaged at educating, equipping, and empowering investors around the world. One of the most common questions we are asked is about which investment is most safe over the long term. For that answer we had industry experts compile the results of a comprehensive study.

THE METHODOLOGY

MEASURING THE INDEXES

We looked at six major categories of investments: the 30-year bond, CDs, gold, silver, the DJIA (Dow), and real estate. For each category we used the price of the underlying asset on the last business day of the year, from 2000 to the end of November 2020. Two decades of statistics removes short-term volatility (huge runups or sell-offs), resulting in a true reflection of growth over time.

MEASURING INFLATION

We use the *real* rate of return on each investment, a calculation that accounts for inflation (the largest hidden tax on all of us). The only true reflection of an asset's safety has to measure how much inflation has eaten into gains on all investments.

But what if the inflation figure used has been corrupted? There is a serious problem with the official inflation rate as measured by the Consumer Price Index (CPI), a Bureau of Labor Statistics (BLS) methodology that tracks price change over time for a preset basket of goods. In 1996 under President Bill Clinton, the calculations became extremely flawed, and are to this day. Explained below are a few of the significant changes implemented, including the ability to substitute which consumer items are used, the statisticians changing from arithmetic to geometric weighting, and how the CPI accounts for quality enhancements made to products—these changes have made measurement of the CPI's basket of goods meaningless.

A lower inflation-rate figure—whether honest or not—helps the government keep more money because inflation-adjusted payments stay lower, which are those funds returned to Americans through outlays for things like Social Security, veteran benefits, federal pensions, and food stamps. So because it is politically expedient, in 1996 they began to allow endless substitutions to that formerly set basket of goods. But how can they measure the true rate of inflation if items can be constantly substituted, literally letting them substitute apples for oranges?

Here is an example of product substitution used to cover up higher inflation: let's say the government's BLS measures the increase in steak prices over time, but then when it goes up too quickly, maybe 20%, they switch to measuring the price of ground beef—a product costing 40% less than steak. That quick change to this one item in the basket of goods would falsely claim that the beef category has seen a *60% reduction* from the true costs, rather than the *20% increase!*

A similar scenario is played out with quality enhancements: let's say the price of unleaded gasoline is up 10%, but a new gasoline additive has just reduced "scary" carbon emissions by 30%. Instead of CPI fuel costs reflecting the true 10% increase— like your wallet does—they would mark down a 30% reduction in cost (not reality) because of the additive's "quality enhancements" to the environment. This is another calculation that makes the measurement meaningless.

These are just a couple examples of the changes in the CPI basket of goods used to measure inflation. Now let's dive deeper into those two, as well as arithmetic versus geometric averaging and why Clinton appointed the Boskin Commission in 1996 to change the methodology. Then we will discuss the importance of knowing the true inflation rate and an inflation-adjusted comparison of the six asset classes composing the vast majority of all investments in America.

QUALITY ADJUSTMENT ISSUES

CPI is steeped in a method of estimating prices called *hedonic demand theory*, something the Boskin Commission referred to as "quality change bias." The commission claimed that product-quality improvements were not accounted for properly in prices, as new or improved products were possibly more efficient and required less maintenance. This pricing method is based on the framework put forth by Griliches (1967) and Rosen (1974). But the major problems with hedonic price adjustments is that they are arbitrary, and do nothing to properly measure the amount that consumers spend on items.

Quality-adjustment problems in the CPI are mostly from new products, so let's first examine *product life cycle theory*. When a new product enters the market, R&D (Research and Development) expenses need to be accounted for into its price, and widespread acceptance will only happen as more consumers become familiar with it over time. Once the public accepts it, sales and profitability lead to competitors entering the marketplace, increasing competition that generally results in the sale price decreasing. Once the market becomes saturated and prices have declined to their lowest possible level, a manufacturer can only gain more market share by increasing their product's perceived value versus the others, which can be attained by adding new features or somehow making the product better. The new features and quality improvements will generally cause an increase in the price. Therefore, the life cycle of newly introduced products will be U-shaped: high initial price, decreasing with competition, and then increasing with product enhancements that allow the item to gain market share (Krumme & Hayter, 1975; Malecki, 1991; Wasson, 1974).

So the CPI's hedonic pricing adjustments attempt to put a price on quality improvements, a method most often utilized with electronics where technology upgrades are called quality improvements. This allows CPI to deduct the arbitrary value given to the improvement, resulting in a lowered price increase than what actually comes out of our pockets to purchase the item. Another example of a hedonic adjustment was seen in the 1990s when air-quality regulations began mandating a gasoline additive to make fuel burning cleaner, causing the consumer cost of gasoline to go up ten cents per gallon. But the CPI logged no price increase; instead, the cost was hedonically adjusted because the perceived benefit of cleaner air was considered a quality improvement worth the ten cents, thus eliminating the price increase in the CPI's basket of goods—though we have paid it out of our pockets ever since (Welling, 2006; Williams, 2004).

ARITHMETIC VERSUS GEOMETRIC AVERAGING

The BLS changed the CPI's weighting from arithmetic to geometric averaging, despite the former being how most people add, subtract, and divide. BLS claimed geometric averaging would approximate the substitution effect by lowering the basket-of-goods weighting on items that have increased in price and raising the weight of items whose price has decreased (Welling, 2006). But the ability to substitute already did damage to the CPI's credibility by underreporting the inflation increase, and now this methodology further underreports price increases.

THE BOSKIN COMMISSION

The intent behind the 1996 Boskin Commission seems benign and grounded in solid theory, but aspects like hedonic price adjustments for quality improvements are already accounted for in other areas of the price index, making the added, artificial lowering of real price increases appear ridiculous for a measurement of true inflation. For example, if a product increases its energy efficiency, then less energy or fuel will be consumed (less demand means prices drop), so the change already shows up elsewhere in the index. The measure of inflation change on a product should be determined by the objective cost of obtaining it—the effect on the consumer's wallet—not the subjective, perceived benefit of owning it.

RESULTS OF THE BOSKIN COMMISSION
RECOMMENDATIONS

Prior to the Boskin Commission changes in 1996, the CPI underweighted new products and overweighted mature ones, an issue that created an *upward* bias in the price index (Boskin, Dulberger, Gordon, Griliches, & Jorgenson, 1996). Because the CPI determines how much to increase or decrease federal payments to approximately fifty million Social Security recipients and twenty million who get food stamps (Baumohl, 2005), the US government can keep more of our money by understating inflation.

John Williams of Gillespie Research (2004) conducted an extensive study comparing geometric weighting with the traditional, arithmetically arrived CPI (pre-1996) and found that geometric understates true inflation by a whopping 2.7% (Williams, 2004). Aggregating that over time, since 1996 this Boskin change has reduced the annual cost-of-living increases to Social Security recipients by 30% (Williams, 2004).

Because of the many obvious and not-so-obvious problems with its new methodology, the Boskin Commission recommendations were squelched from rightful concerns that the new CPI basket of goods would not reflect actual prices (Williams, 2004). But that resistance became irrelevant during the Clinton administration, when the BLS quietly began changing the index on their own, without congressional approval (Williams, 2004). Thus, through techniques like product substitution, quality price adjustments, and geometric versus arithmetic averaging, the commission was able to greatly reduce the perceived inflation rate reported by the CPI.

HOW DO WE MEASURE INFLATION IN THIS EXHAUSTIVE RESEARCH?

Contrary to that convoluted and corrupted methodology, our unofficial measurement of inflation simply reflects how much people spend on products over time. Those amounts are easily tracked by simply determining how much of GDP (Gross Domestic Product) is consumer spending, and then measuring the amount spent in each category, such as automobiles, fuel, food, and clothing. These costs are easily found through the price recorded on each item by its associated trade organization.

What was our final result? From 2000 to 2020, the true rate of inflation has averaged 185% higher—per year—than what has been claimed by the post-1996 official CPI.

WHICH ASSET CLASS IS BEST?

Shocking implications from our analysis: By late 2020, though the stock market was near an all-time high, its annualized growth per year over the two decades—after deducting the *true* inflation rate—has averaged *less* than 1% (0.93%). During the same period, silver and gold were by far the best investments, almost *tripling* the stock market's growth. And the other three asset categories (bonds, CDs, real estate) showed negative earnings after accounting for inflation.

Figure A below summarizes our research, and Figure B details the per-year results for each asset class since 2000.

The story behind the numbers is important to understand because each number demonstrates the intersection of fiscal and monetary policies, political trends, geo-political conflict, the interest rate cycle, the impending debt crisis, unemployment, and demographic trends. To preserve and even increase savings, today's inflation requires us to take advantage of the trends—so the trends don't take advantage of us.

FIGURE A: BRIEF SUMMARY OF THE 20 YEAR COMPARATIVE ANALYSIS

	% OF TIME RETURN > INFLATION	ANNUAL AVERAGE	ANNUALIZED AFTER INFLATION
BONDS	19%	3.06%	-1.84%
GOLD	57%	8.32%	2.39%
SILVER	48%	9.2%	3.27%
STOCKS	48%	6.86%	0.93%
CD	5%	1.61%	-4.2%
REAL ESTATE	43%	3.69%	-2.24%

FIGURE B: YEAR BY YEAR ASSET ANALYSIS OF THE RESEARCH

	30 YEAR BOND	CD	GOLD		SILVER		DJIA		REAL ESTATE		CPI	REAL INFLATION
2000	6.63%	5.01%	$289	1.00%	$5.10	-0.58%	11,239.98	20.17%	$165,300	5.02%	3.40%	9.70%
2001	5.54%	5.33%	$268	-7.18%	$4.52	-11.37 %	10,659.26	-5.17%	$169,800	2.72%	2.80%	7.99%
2002	5.45%	2.14%	$278	3.77%	$4.72	4.42%	9,876.68	-7.34%	$188,700	11.13%	1.60%	4.57%
2003		1.47%	$347	24.94%	$4.84	2.54%	8,389.13	-15.06%	$186,000	-1.43%	2.30%	6.56%
2004		1.15%	$422	21.66%	$6.22	28.51%	10,528.94	25.51%	$212,700	14.35%	2.70%	7.70%
2005		2.08%	$436	3.13%	$6.47	4.02%	10,539.66	0.10%	$232,500	9.31%	3.40%	9.70%
2006		3.28%	$513	17.77%	$8.95	38.33%	10,857.48	3.02%	$247,700	6.54%	3.20%	9.13%
2007	4.85%	3.78%	$632	23.20%	$12.88	43.91%	12,565.33	15.73%	$257,400	3.92%	2.80%	7.99%
2008	4.33%	3.51%	$833	31.80%	$14.80	14.91%	12,413.99	-1.20%	$233,900	-9.13%	3.80%	10.84%
2009	3.13%	1.79%	$870	4.41%	$10.97	-25.88%	8,239.70	-33.63%	$208,400	-10.90%	-0.40%	-1.14%
2010	4.60%	0.81%	$1,088	25.04%	$18.64	69.92%	10,296.09	24.96%	$222,900	6.96%	1.60%	4.57%
2011	4.52%	0.48%	$1,406	29.24%	$28.31	51.88%	12,241.21	18.89%	$226,900	1.79%	3.20%	9.13%
2012	3.03%	0.34%	$1,598	13.70%	$33.72	19.11%	12,605.03	2.97%	$238,400	5.07%	2.10%	5.99%
2013	3.08%	0.28%	$1,658	3.72%	$31.11	-7.74%	13,760.98	9.17%	$258,400	8.39%	1.50%	4.28%
2014	3.77%	0.23%	$1,205	-27.33%	$20.39	-34.46 %	16,118.39	17.13%	$275,200	6.50%	1.60%	4.57%
2015	2.46%	0.27%	$1,206	0.12%	$16.54	-18.88%	17,521.62	8.71%	$296,500	7.74%	0.10%	0.29%
2016	2.86%	0.27%	$1,060	-12.11%	$13.86	-16.20 %	16,219.86	-7.43%	$312,800	5.50%	1.30%	3.71%
2017	3.02%	0.36%	$1,229	15.94%	$16.22	17.03%	22,000.00	35.64%	$313,100	0.10%	1.60%	4.57%
2018	3.10%	0.33%	$1,281	4.23%	$15.46	-4.69%	23,062.40	4.83%	$362,400	4.00%	1.90%	5.42%
2019	2.58%	0.53%	$1,515	18.20%	$17.88	15.70%	28,462.14	23.40%	$312,500	-13.76%	2.30%	6.55%
2020 YTD	1.39%	0.28%	$1,918	26.60%	$25.10	40.40%	29,520.00	3.70%	$322,340	3.14%	1.00%	2.55%
SUM	64.34%	33.72%		177.06%		174.78%		144.10%		77.57%	43.80%	124.66%
Annual Average Adjusted	3.06%	1.61%		8.32%		9.20%		6.86%		3.69%	2.08%	5.93%
Return	-1.84%	-4.20%		2.39%		3.27		0.93%		-2.24%		

Chapter 6

OWNING SILVER

THE OPPORTUNITY OF A LIFETIME

We are rarely given the opportunity to invest in a truly significant bull market, but right now we're witnessing one that will yield enormous gains, rewarding savvy investors for many years to come. During the early 1970s to 1980, silver soared from $1.50 to

$50 per ounce, a 3,300% move. That means a $25,000 investment in silver at $1.50 per ounce soared to over $825,000 by 1980.

Today the silver fundamentals are stronger than any time since 1971. In fact, silver is perhaps the most undervalued asset in the world. An enormous supply-versus-demand shortfall has developed in the precious metal, and unlike the 1970s there is no longer a huge, above-ground supply available. With a much more limited global silver supply, the amount waiting to be purchased has been evaporating over the past few years and will continue to disappear.

For decades, the price of silver and gold have been artificially suppressed by central banks, governments, wealthy speculators, and even the mines themselves. Through a complex series of silver leases, sales, and derivatives, a global short position (a market bet that the price will go down) of two billion ounces in *paper silver* (shorting the electronic-stock price of silver instead of selling real, physical silver) has been created, by far the largest silver short in history. As these different entities run out of available silver to cover their short bets, a massive short squeeze is likely to develop, which will propel the price of silver to historic levels.

Over the past twenty years, I have recommended customers maintain a silver-coin position to hedge again fiat currency and provide a survival asset in the event of crisis. Today I am also advising silver for its profit potential.

WAYS TO OWN SILVER

US-circulated 90%-silver coins are traded in bags of $1000 face value and contain approximately 715 ounces of silver.

US-circulated silver dollar bags contain 1000 circulated US Peace dollars, which are over seventy-five years old and in very good condition. A full bag is about 770 ounces of silver. Circulated silver dollars are considered collectible, so they have a higher premium than bullion coins and bars.

For investors interested in upscale silver collectibles, popular investment-grade silver dollars are certified MS63 to MS69 Peace and Morgan dollars. Semi-numismatic coins generally range in condition from lightly circulated to MS65. The semi-numismatic level of collectible coins falls into the category between bullion and numismatic. In the next chapter on gold, I will give a more detailed explanation of the different values for categories of coins. But for now keep in mind that collectible coins which once traded at five to ten times the silver price no longer bring the same levels of premium over the silver price: markets have changed, including the addition of cryptocurrencies as a potential investment, so those returns will probably never be seen again.

One-ounce American Silver Eagle dollars are dated from their inception in 1986 through current mintage in 2022. At 0.999 pure silver, they are minted in West Point, New York, and normally sell for modest premiums above their melt value.

Also at 0.999 pure silver, one of the most widely traded silver-bullion coins on the market today are Canadian Silver Maple Leafs. If you are considering a government-minted bullion coin, this is generally less expensive than the US Silver Eagle, but significantly more costly than a one-ounce silver *round*.

Silver *bars* come in ten-, one hundred-, and one thousand-ounce sizes. The thousand-ounce bars are non-assayed, meaning none of them are guaranteed to be exactly that size. However, you only pay for the number of ounces in any particular bar. For example, a bar weight may be something like 998.772 ounces if it is a "light bar" or 1021.881 ounces if it is a "heavy bar."

Silver bullion *rounds* are a popular, low-premium way to invest in silver. They offer the best of three worlds: they are 0.999 pure, they're the lowest cost of the one-ounce coins, and the one-ounce size makes

them easily used as money in a worst-case scenario of societal breakdown.

TYPES OF SILVER COINS AND BARS

AMERICAN EAGLE	CANADIAN MAPLE LEAF	COMEX APPROVED BAR

TYPES OF SILVER COINS AND BARS

"PEACE" SILVER DOLLAR	MORGAN SILVER DOLLAR	PRE-1965 90% "JUNK" SILVER
Minted: 1921-1935	Minted 1878-1904; 1921	Minted: 1964 and earlier

Generally, during times of economic slowdown, industrial metals like silver, copper, steel, iron, and aluminum will see their prices fall as manufacturing demand for these metals decreases. But even though silver is an industrial metal—used in almost all electronics—it is also a financial metal like gold. Both are used as money.

WHAT DO FINANCIAL METALS RESPOND TO?

During chaos, uncertainty, turbulence, turmoil, and change, financial metals act as safe-haven investments. As things become more uncertain, a flight to quality occurs, meaning investors gravitate out of risky assets and into safe, tangible assets that hold their value. Today's financial situation has been getting worse and worse as central banks around the world print money without discretion to stimulate their economies. This continues to create massive inflation. Europe is on the verge of complete collapse, the Middle East is becoming more dangerous with each passing day, and America has amassed so much debt that it is impossible to pay back.

But not all hope is lost during this unfolding global economic catastrophe. In fact, these exact conditions are what cause gold and silver to skyrocket as investors reassess their risk profile, get out of risky investments, and allocate into safe assets. This is where silver acts like gold with its financial characteristics beginning to outweigh its industrial use. Again, right now silver is possibly the most undervalued asset on the planet, making it the opportunity of a lifetime. As such, it needs to be a large part of everyone's financial portfolio—for protection, preservation, *and* growth.

CHAPTER 7

OWNING GOLD

For the past 6000 years, the most sought-after form of asset protection has been gold, and gold coins are the most liquid financial asset in the world, having no borders, being recognized throughout the world, and being easily hidden or transported. For these reasons, owning gold represents financial privacy and independence. Gold frustrates the attempts of governments to completely control the finances and lives of its citizens.

WHAT IS CURRENCY AND HOW DOES IT DIE?

The dictionary definition of *currency* is "something that is used as a medium of exchange; money; the fact or quality of being widely accepted and circulated from person to person."[21] History repeatedly warns that all fiat currencies (currencies that have no tangible backing by real commodities with intrinsic value) inevitably die; they have a 0% life expectancy in the long run.

According to a study conducted by dollardaze.org, of 775 fiat currencies they looked at, the average lasted only twenty-seven years, with the shortest making it one month.

Though the longest-lasting currency has been the British pound sterling (at over 300 years), during its time of being printed without discretion—since it was taken off any tangible backing—the pound sterling has lost 99.5% of its value. A similar story happened when the US dollar was taken off the gold standard in 1971, making it a fiat currency. Over the next forty-two years our American currency lost 99% of its value.

This is why people need gold! First and foremost, the yellow money should be viewed as an insurance policy against a collapsing currency—against *all* fiat currencies. Gold maintains its purchasing power over time. As I detail more in Chapter 9, during the 1920s, $20 or an ounce of gold would buy a quality men's suit with all the accessories. As of this writing, a $1700 ounce of gold will still buy the same suit and then some, while $20 buys average dress socks. Right now, because of global political and economic conditions, securing your assets from loss means buying gold and silver for preservation and protection. A popular phrase during the Great Depression was "cash was king," but that's misleading because the US dollar was backed by gold at that time, so the king was gold.

Besides being an excellent insurance, gold is also a fantastic investment. While most assets dropped like a stone in the 1930s, the price of gold shot up dramatically. During a depression, economic crisis, inflation, or war, people seek financial security, and that does not include investing in paper assets that only *promise* to pay. Instead, people become more and more drawn to gold and silver coins that store value no matter what happens. Precious metals generally respond poorly to flourishing economic news, but on the flip side they normally perform well as societies get worse politically and economically.

Gyrating economies swinging from inflation to deflation make traditional paper-investment strategies obsolete, meaning gold coins or bars should be a major part of every investor's portfolio over these financially turbulent years for the US and the world. Whether you want to invest in gold *or* silver at any given time will depend of the current ratio between the two metals. But either one is preferred over fiat currency at times like these when America has taken on too much debt and has too little revenue, putting the dollar in a *long-term* bear market. The US dollar recently had a substantial rise in value, but only in relation to the other fiat currencies failing around the world.

As the US dollar continues its long-term trend down and away from being a secure reserve currency—and losing most of its buying power over time—millions of foreigners will redirect their money out of US dollars and into precious metals, the money that always retains its buying power. And all it would take to spark an explosion in the price of gold and silver is one major event, like an escalation of terrorism on US soil, an expansion of the war in the Middle East, another stock market meltdown, or a major bank failure.

As consumer prices accelerate higher, at any point panic buying of precious metals can begin. And those that neglected tangible assets will miss the opportunity for profits from exploding metals prices, while seeing their fiat paper currency lose more and more value. To safeguard your financial portfolio, your paper assets should be hedged (balanced) with precious metals. Over time, the recommended percentage of your portfolio allocated into precious metals will depend on how bad economic conditions are.

During the 1980s and 1990s when most asset classes were booming, gold and silver dropped in value, so having 50% of your financial portfolio allocated into precious metals would have been a mistake. But when facing hyperinflation like the entire world is today, having 50% in metals is probably too little during our immediate future when gold, silver, and other tangible assets will likely be the only assets to maintain value.

So the recommended percentage allocated into precious metals is dynamic, changing with world conditions. Generally, as an economy improves, you want to lock in profits and reduce your holdings of precious metals, but then as a nation's finances get worse, you want to add to your metals position. Times change and so should your investment strategy; a "buy and hold forever" strategy is a horrible methodology because nothing goes up or down forever.

Through constant economic change, one warning must be kept in mind: society gets ugly quickly when people cannot afford food, clothing, fuel, or shelter. In order to trade for those necessities, people will want anything with value, and physical precious metals offer exactly what is needed for sustained purchasing power—something recognizable, valuable, and portable.

Gold and silver ETF (Exchange Traded Fund) stocks fail to be reliable precious metals investments because they are just more paper promises. And shares of gold and silver mining companies are stocks that also carry volatility risk: miners can lose a lot of value quickly and even go out of business. But physical gold and silver have always been worth something. Taking physical possession of gold and silver coins and bars—also storing some with a reputable facility if needed—is the safest way to invest in precious metals. In fact, all other methods of owning metals involve holding paper promises.

GOLD INVESTMENT

Now let's look at the pros and cons for each type of physical gold you can invest in. There are three categories of gold coins: bullion, numismatic, and semi-numismatic. Bullion coins are purchased primarily for the physical melt value of the gold or silver ounces. They are minted by major governments but are not intended to be used in circulation. They offer a way to invest directly in the different precious metals at only a slight premium over their metal content. Bullion coins are quite liquid and easy to track.

BULLION COINS

GOLD AMERICAN EAGLE   SOUTH AFRICAN KRUGERRAND   CANADIAN MAPLE LEAF

NUMISMATIC COINS

The word "numismatic" is derived from the Latin word *numisma*, which means "coin." Numismatic coins are the opposite end of the gold-coin spectrum from bullion coins. Numismatic coins were legal tender minted decades earlier and now exist in limited supply. These are collector coins that are not desirable for the average person to invest in because of the excessive premiums and commissions. The value of a numismatic coin is based on its rarity, age, condition, and demand in the marketplace. My recommendation is to always buy bullion so that you maximize the ounces you own—a key to wealth accumulation.

The prices of numismatic coins are derived much differently from bullion coins, for which scarcity and market demand have little to do with the price. Bullion price sticks close to the "spot" (market) price of the metal ounces in the coin, though dealer margins can increase with any amount of temporary or extended scarcity. Most rare numismatic coins are purchased in higher grades, such as MS66 to MS70. This category would include extremely rare, museum-quality, US and foreign gold coins.

SEMI-NUMISMATIC COINS

Semi-numismatic coins are a category that falls between bullion and numismatic. These coins are not as rare and expensive as numismatic coins. Semi-numismatic coins generally range in condition from lightly circulated to MS65. The commissions on semi-numismatic coins are much lower than on numismatic coins, and semis offer investors greater liquidity. Again, nothing goes up or down forever, so you want to eventually lock in profits by selling your gold, meaning your investments must be liquid. Like numismatic coins, semi-numismatic coins are not automatically liquid, so be sure yours will have a market of people who want it when you decide to sell—your exit strategy is just as important as your entry through a purchase.

Like numismatic coins, semi-numismatic coins are investment-grade coins. However, semis can be purchased at lower prices than numismatic coins, though even semis are substantially more expensive per ounce than bullion coins.

EXAMPLES OF SEMI-NUMISMATIC COINS

LIBERTY $20 DOUBLE EAGLE — Minted 1877-1907

ST. GAUDENS $20 DOUBLE EAGLE — Minted 1907-1933

EUROPEAN GOLD COINS

It is my opinion that semi-numismatic European gold coins should not be purchased because bullion gold is much less expensive *per ounce*. Though European gold coins are a popular option with gold investors, they are old and some *may* have relatively low premiums that are only slightly higher than modern bullion; however, per ounce most of them are substantially more expensive than bullion coins. At fractions of an ounce, European gold coins are normally the size of a US dime, nickel, or quarter. Consider these aspects when purchasing European gold coins:

1. Stick with those that are easily recognized from well-known countries, allowing you a well-established market when it comes time to sell them.

2. Do not buy restrikes, which are bullion coins like the Swiss and French 20 francs or Austrian gold coins that exhibit older dates but were actually minted many years after the date that appears on the coins.

3. Stick with low mintages. For collector appeal, a coin must have some scarcity so the number of coins originally minted should not be astronomical.

4. Buy only uncirculated coins because collectors and investors are drawn to an attractive, higher-grade coin. Seek out coins that were most likely hidden away in bank vaults so they were never released for public circulation.

5. Buy those of significant age. Like any true collectible, age matters. A piece of furniture made in the past ten years does not qualify as an antique, and the same applies to coins. Those minted in the past few years have little collector appeal.

6. Buy fractional sizes. Most European gold coins are ¼ ounce or smaller, which makes sense because they were once used as money. Their small, fractional size is especially convenient when it comes time to transport, sell, barter, or liquidate the coins.

EXAMPLES OF EUROPEAN GOLD COINS
BRITISH SOVEREIGN KING   FRENCH 20 FRANC NAPOLEON III   DUTCH GUILDER "QUEEN"
BELGIUM 20 FRANC   ITALIAN 20 LIRE   SWEDISH 20 KRONER

MINT STATE (MS) GRADING OF RARE COINS

All graded coins go through an MS process:

1. Whenever an ungraded coin is found, it is said to begin the process in its "raw" state.

2. The coin is then sent to a grading company where a panel of "numismatists" (gold coin experts) grade the coin, giving it an MS designation.

3. The coin is then placed in a sealed case and given a serial number to verify its authenticity.

From that process of registering a coin, we can know the grade given to your coin, the ongoing number of those coins that have been graded, and their total population, meaning how many have been minted and put into circulation.

Looking at the range of MS designations, if a coin is graded and uncirculated, it will range from MS60 to MS70. MS60 is the lowest grade of uncirculated coins, but that does not mean low quality because it is still uncirculated and in mint condition. MS70 is a perfect specimen of the highest grade and obviously uncirculated. Even at five times magnification, MS70s will show no marks of any kind, so they are museum quality coins that fetch an incredibly high price.

Anything below an MS60 designation means the coin was circulated, so it got scratched and otherwise abused while in cash registers, purses, change jars, and pockets. Circulated coins are great for acquiring ounces of gold at low prices, whereas uncirculated coins gain in value when premiums (a cost over the spot price of the metal) increase with more demand, giving the investor increased value on their investment. That is the sales pitch you will hear from dealers who sell uncirculated coins at high premiums and commissions. But unless you are a collector, these should not be a part of your investment portfolio.

BUYER BEWARE

Not all grading companies are the same: some unethical people deceptively grade coins with a false MS designation—the precious metals industry is *not* regulated. Though there are dozens of companies that grade coins, I am only comfortable purchasing from Professional Coin Grading Service (PCGS) and Numismatic Guaranty Company (NGC). With MS grading and any other aspect of the unregulated metals industry, always keep your guard up against possibly unreputable dealers.

FREQUENTLY ASKED QUESTIONS

Before buying a coin as an investment, you need to know if that coin matches your investment goals. One of the most important considerations is how easily you will be able to sell the coin later— how desirable and liquid it is. With that in mind, here are some questions to ask:

1. *When was the coin minted?* After 1933, the US and the rest of the world stopped minting gold coins as legal tender. However, some gold coins were later reproduced by countries reusing their old dies (imprint stamping tools). As mentioned earlier, these coins are known as "restrikes" and should be avoided. Swiss and French 20 francs were re-produced in the mid-1940s using old die casts with much earlier dates. Bearing the date 1915, Austrian ducats are even *currently* being reproduced; yet, they are offered as old coins that sell for a premium. This sort of restriking keeps coins from being considered collectible because no one knows

the actual number minted on a certain date, nor which are new or old.

2. *Is the coin protected from confiscation?* In 1933, President Franklin D. Roosevelt set a US precedent when he instituted executive orders outlawing the ownership of gold, except for jewelry and collectible coins. My opinion is that this will never happen again in the US because gold and silver are no longer fungible (they are not used as currency). Also, the confiscation would be unfruitful since less than 2% of Americans own gold and under 1% have silver. As the US financial crisis worsens, our government will most likely confiscate people's assets, but it will probably be done via the stroke of a pen with bail-ins at the banks and capital gains taxes.

3. A collectible coin is often promoted as being far less likely to be confiscated because of the government's previous exclusion; even when Stalin and Hitler confiscated gold, they did not take collectible coins. But less than 5% of Americans own gold in the form of collectible coins, so it is simply not worth it for our government to start confiscating coin collections. However, the government can do whatever they want—often with no regard for the US Constitution—so we must not fall into the trap of counting on old, rare, or semi-rare coins that might allow us to avoid confiscation. Today much less expensive bullion is as unlikely to be confiscated as rare or semi-rare coins.

4. *Do you have an exit strategy?* Too often investors purchase metals without considering how and when to sell them. I have invested countless hours planning and formulating my own exit strategy, and our investment advisors can help you incorporate this critical step in your financial planning.

5. *Will the coin help protect your privacy?* It is important to note that *dealer* non-reportable does not mean *tax* non-reportable. The dealer is not required to report anything about you when selling you precious metals, but whenever you sell those metals and have a gain or loss, it must be reported on your tax return.

6. *Does the coin have upside potential?* Bullion coins move up in value only when the spot price of gold and silver move up. Again, semi-numismatic coins get their value both from their gold content and rarity, giving them a double play in both the

bullion and rare-coin markets; however, over more than the past two decades, premium advances on rare coins have not been seen. Knowing that, I suggest you *never* purchase a semi-numismatic or numismatic gold or silver coin—*only buy bullion.*

7. Is the dealer reputable? Many coins are sold through local coin shops where the dealers cater to hobbyists and generally lack experience in building sound investment portfolios. Also, most small coin shops are not equipped to handle large purchases.

CHAPTER 8

HOW NATIONS DIE

LESSONS FROM HISTORY, INCLUDING THE FALL OF ROME, VENEZUELA, ARGENTINA, AND TODAY'S AMERICA

IT ALL STARTS WITH AN ABSENCE OF CHARACTER

No society that has lost character can keep liberty. What follows is chaos and tyranny. Economic prosperity is achieved by nations that have individual liberty, something that takes hold through people of courage, justice, self-control, and prudence. Expansion of individual liberty happens when nations incorporate a separation of powers, a system of checks and balances, and protection of certain rights (for at least most citizens).[22, 23]

When the Roman republic fell into a dictatorship, 33% of all Romans were receiving public relief.[24] How does that compare to modern day America? Sadly, we are much worse. Here are the states and amounts people can bring in by receiving a year of welfare payments, bringing citizens more money than they would have made working a full-time, minimum wage job-leaving residents little reason to take entry-level employment:

Hawaii $60,590
D.C. $50,820
Massachusetts $50,540
Connecticut $44,370
New York $44,370

New Jersey $43,450
Rhode Island $43,330
Vermont $42,350
New Hampshire $39,750
Maryland $38,160
California $37,160
Oregon $34,300
Wyoming $32,620
Nevada $29,820
Minnesota $29,350
Delaware $29,220
Washington $28,840
North Dakota $28,830
Pennsylvania $28,670
New Mexico $27,900
Montana $26,930
South Dakota $26,610
Kansas $26,490
Michigan $26,430
Alaska $26,400
Ohio $26,200
North Carolina $25,760
West Virginia $24,900
Alabama $23,310
Indiana $22,900
Missouri $22,800
Oklahoma $22,480
Louisiana $22,250 [25]

Other warning signs we see in America that similarly happened during the Roman republic's erosion are an overextended military, a purposely debased currency to pay off debts, a massive bureaucracy parasitically living off the people's labor, and a loss of control over national borders.

SOME THINGS NEVER CHANGE

In Rome, ideological differences caused the Christian Church to implode, thus weakening the entire nation. Chaldean, Coptic, and Nestorian Christians were unwilling to work with each other against the Muslims. It got so bad that some sects of Christians began working with the Islamic enemy to help marginalize other Christians, allowing the intruding Islamic caliphate to eventually take control over all Christians.

Like many of us today, maybe the different groups of believers felt they were each the only *real* Christians, so they would not help the others. God's people are often destroyed from their own stupid choices. It also could have been that a group or two of the Christians sold their souls to the enemy in exchange for power, but that normally does not end well and ultimately the Roman Christians were defeated. The church walked away from the biblical truth laid out in God's blueprint for a successful life: God's Word with its commandments and statutes were not given to mankind to control us—Scripture sets us free!

TEMPTATIONS OF THE WELFARE STATE

"The absence of character produces chaos and tyranny. When Romans allowed the temptations of the welfare state to erode their character; abandoned responsibility and self-discipline, self-reliance, and respect for the property of others; and began to use government to rob Peter to pay Paul, they turned down a fateful and destructive path."[26]

From there a nation normally loses its soul, part of which involves the citizens demanding that government take care of them with free food, healthcare, and retirement income. They vote out politicians who will not give them what they want. The first chart in chapter 3 shows the proposed 2022 US budget. It tells us that total, federal revenue for 2022 is expected to be $4.17 trillion. But federal spending, entitlements, and mandatory payments take 96% of that revenue. Then if you add interest owed on our national debt, we are set to spend $4.32 trillion, just on Social Security, Medicare, Medicaid, other mandatory programs, and interest—a total of 3% more than expected revenue. However, all US federal spending for 2022 will come out to $6.01 trillion, which gives us new 2022 debt of $1.84 trillion. Adding that onto what we already owe, our accumulated national debt will be $30.5 trillion.

If we remove seven zeros from those numbers above, we can demonstrate the US financial situation in terms of the same year, 2022, for just one high-income household:

Family income: $417,000

Spending: $601,000

New debt on credit cards: $184,000

Outstanding balance on credit cards by the end of 2022: $3,050,000

Massive US government handouts each year drive up national deficits, even while handouts are harmful to people's desire to work, earn, and feel good about being productive. Though Disney World accepts their extensive share of government handouts, at least they seem to understand the problem with handouts when it comes to animals. On a recent family vacation there, we noticed this sign while waiting in line to go on the Kilimanjaro Safaris ride:

"Never attempt to feed the animals. They are wild creatures with natural diets and should not be made dependent on handouts."

FERTILITY RATES AND FINANCIAL TROUBLE GO HAND AND HAND

From the above US budget, you can see how it is impossible for America to balance its federal budget unless entitlements are slashed. And this issue is not just a problem for the United States: entitlements are a global ticking time bomb. And one of the scariest trends in world history is modern-day fertility rates, something outlined in Dr. James Dobson's three-book series: *Fatherless, Childless,* and *Godless.* Once you see the problem, you will realize that the global economy cannot recover for at least a generation, and that is only if drastic change is immediately enacted worldwide—which will not happen.

For a nation to grow, the fertility rate needs to be greater than two children birthed for every two parents. Society shrinks when two adults die and have not been replaced by at least two children.

So a devastating fertility rate is anything below two because it means the country is aging. A higher and higher percentage of people will be entering retirement years and receiving benefits—without paying anything *more* into the system. National entitlements are mostly Ponzi schemes because the entire system eventually collapses when there are not enough people paying into the system for the total amount of benefits being paid out to non-workers. As shown on in the chart in chapter 3, here are the present birthrates for the most powerful countries in the world:

France: 2.0

United Kingdom: 2.0

United States: 1.9

Norway: 1.9

Australia: 1.9

Sweden: 1.9

Brazil: 1.8

Iran: 1.6

Canada: 1.6

China: 1.6

Russia: 1.5

Switzerland: 1.5

Japan: 1.4

Germany: 1.4

Italy: 1.4

Singapore: 1.2

Again, even if policies were enacted to entice people to have as many kids as possible, the birthrate problem cannot be fixed for at least a generation. The global economy does not have that much time before the worldwide entitlement time bomb explodes, causing a hyperinflationary recession around the world. So the planet's governments must inflate their money supply—or die. There is no other outcome.

Our current White House resident claims the economy is growing and creating jobs, so we can rest easy, right? No. Again, as mentioned in Chapter 3, the equivalent of the entire population of nineteen states is unemployed—24 million working-age US citizens. The total number of Americans not in the labor force is almost

100 million (98,980,000) out of 335 million US citizens. It is scary to think of how quickly the welfare state can bring down a sturdy and industrious people, causing an honorable nation to lose its character. Here are a few truths about the welfare state:

"When a self-governing people confer upon their government the power to take from some and give to others, the process will not stop until the last bone of the last taxpayer is picked bare."[27]

"Government can give only what it first takes."[28]

"There is a reluctance by politicians to cut off the hand that feeds them, and few people will actually bite the hand that feeds them."[29]

Alexander Hamilton said:

"Power over a man's subsistence is power over his will."[30]

WHAT HAPPENED IN THE ROMAN REPUBLIC WHEN THEY PLUNGED INTO A WELFARE STATE?

Civil wars to control the public loot, mass corruption, huge bureaucracy, high taxes, burdensome regulations, and businesses were called upon to support the growing body of public parasites.[30] Sound familiar? It should. History repeats. Edmond Burke once said:

"People will not look forward to prosperity who never look backward to their ancestors."[31]

The modern-day translation would be:

"Those who don't know history are doomed to repeat it."

Lessons from the beginning of the end for ancient Rome:

"In time, the State became the prime source of income for most people. The high taxes needed to finance the State drove business into bankruptcy and then nationalization. Whole sectors of the economy came under government control in this manner. Priests and intellectuals extolled the virtues of the almighty emperor, the Provider of all things. The interests of the individual were considered a distant second to the interests of the emperor and his legions."[32]

This leads to the result of all welfare states: debasement of the currency.

> *"The massive demands on the government to spend for this and that created pressures for the creation of new money. The Roman coin, the denarius, was cheapened and debased by one emperor after another to pay for the expensive programs."*[33]

> *"Once 94% silver, the denarius, by 268 A.D., was little more than a piece of junk containing only.02% silver."*[34]

That is a 99.98% decrease in the value of the currency. In comparison, how much has our US dollar been devalued? Through inflation since the Federal Reserve was created in 1913, the dollar has lost 99% of its purchasing power.

In 1913 dollars, one US dollar today is worth a paltry one cent. However, since this deterioration has taken one hundred years, the American populace has been mostly unaware of the extent to which the dollar's purchasing power has been depleted.

INFLATION'S IMPLICATIONS TO DEMOCRACY

Like the previous paragraph, some of this is repeated in another chapter, but because of its importance we will quickly cover it again: Imagine what it would be like to realize a decline of 98% of retirement assets (life savings) in a month, a week, or even a day. The following chart of the US monetary base shows that money creation has gone parabolic, meaning hyperinflation for America is imminent:

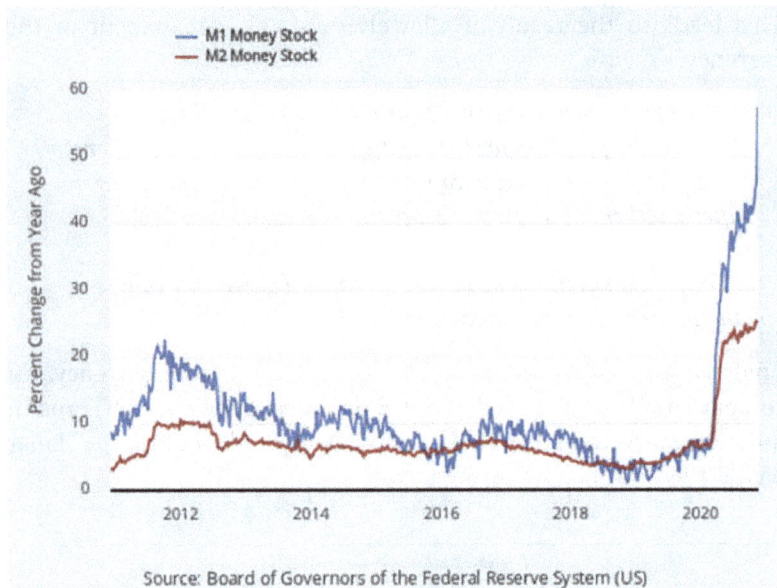

Source: Board of Governors of the Federal Reserve System (US)

How will hyperinflation impact your lifestyle? Asset prices will go through the roof and wages will not keep up with increased prices; thus, it *will* wipe out anyone who is not hedged with tangible assets like gold and silver. This kind of economic catastrophe will lead to a political revolution that takes away our religious, personal, economic, and political freedoms. Do you see any of these eroding already? Yes, it's already happening! The time to prepare is now! Our currency will be wiped out, which will lead to major trade imbalances. And when debtor countries—like the US—begin to default on financial obligations, creditors become extremely upset, often leading to war.

CASE STUDY: VENEZUELA

After Venezuelan President Hugo Chavez's death on March 5, 2013, the bolivar lost 56% of its value. This brought about high inflation. The government responded by imposing ever tougher price controls in an attempt to suppress inflation.[35, 36] To provide stimulus for a collapsing economy, his successor Nicolás Maduro adopted an inflationary policy that increased stimulus (money printing) to $900 million weekly. This caused official prices to soar 49.4%, and retailers were forced to raise their prices in response as their cost of goods purchased for resale went through the roof. [37, 38]

Socialist Venezuela: Business forced to lower prices to be 'fair' or face arrest

See also Government Topics / Venezuela / Socialism / Communism / Class Warfare

November 11, 2013

In Venezuela, Socialist President Nicolás Maduro, who previously served as vice president under Hugo Chávez, has stationed armed national guardsmen "around outlets of an electronics chain [Daka] that Maduro has ordered to lower prices or face prosecution," as reported today by Girish Gupta of USA Today.

Renee Nal
Tampa Conservative Examiner

The slide in the value of the currency caused inflation to soar. Remember, the US dollar has lost 99% of its value since 1913. Venezuela's official level was 49.4% inflation, but the more accurate unofficial amount was around 300%.[39]

The rising prices were due to irresponsible government money printing. Sound familiar? How did the Venezuelan government respond? Maduro accused:

"rich businessmen and right-wing political foes backed by Washington of waging an economic 'war' against him…" and "[threatened] to force more stores to sell their merchandise at cut-rate prices…"[40]

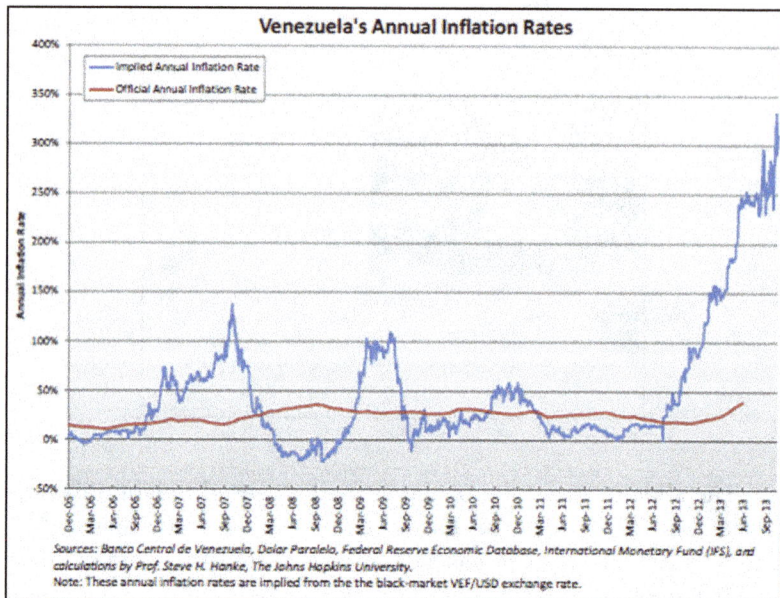

Venezuela's Annual Inflation Rates

Sources: Banco Central de Venezuela, Dolar Paralelo, Federal Reserve Economic Database, International Monetary Fund (IFS), and calculations by Prof. Steve H. Hanke, The Johns Hopkins University.
Note: These annual inflation rates are implied from the the black-market VEF/USD exchange rate.

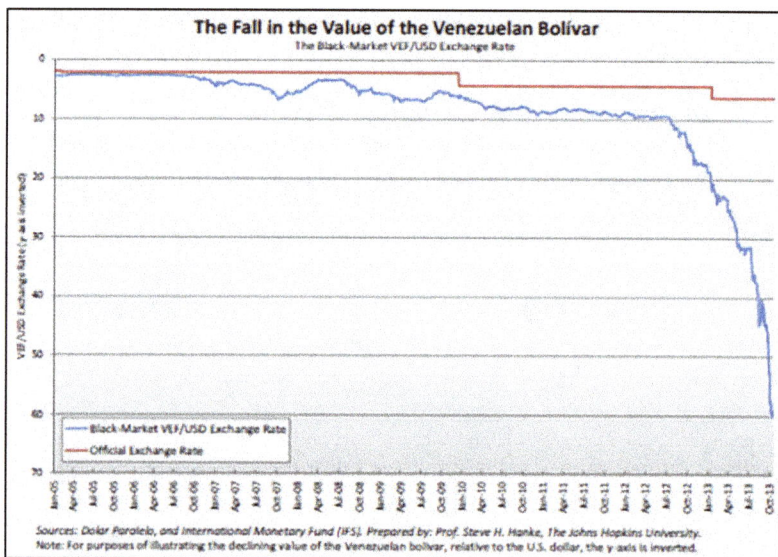

The Fall in the Value of the Venezuelan Bolívar
The Black-Market VEF/USD Exchange Rate

Sources: Dolar Paralelo, and International Monetary Fund (IFS). Prepared by: Prof. Steve H. Hanke, The Johns Hopkins University.
Note: For purposes of illustrating the declining value of the Venezuelan bolívar, relative to the U.S. dollar, the y-axis is inverted.

CASE STUDY: ARGENTINA

Not yet ten years ago in Argentina, prices began soaring, foreign reserves were falling, and the peso had its sharpest slide in twelve years. Instead of rioting, Argentines fell back on tried-and-true survival skills learned in earlier, turbulent times. Here's an example: With inflation at about 30%, Sofia Basualdo, a 43-year-old geography teacher, used shopping sprees to beat further price rises. Leaving a Buenos Aires supermarket and pushing a cart filled to the brim, Basualdo explains:

"I might pay one peso for a product today, but next week I'll likely have to pay two pesos..."[41]

CAUSE AND EFFECT

Argentinian inflation was hovering at about 30% annually, but accelerating rapidly. The government's erratic decision-making was the biggest risk looming over the volatile peso, as the policies that triggered the currency crunch only became more contradictory during the unfolding crisis. Due to uncertainty over public policy that was meant to attack the crisis, the Argentinian peso fell 15% in just the last week of January 2014.[42] A 15% devaluation in one week! That's not even the worst of it. The last two months of 2013, the Argentinian peso collapsed 30%, then stabilized for about a year, until one day in 2015 it dropped another 29%. Remember, money that no one wants will continue to come down.[43]

Unfortunately the Argentines had not learned from a previous currency crisis that occurred in 2001. At that time their peso lost 70% of its value, creating riots and social unrest. Banks froze deposits and barricaded behind sheet metal as thousands of protesters unsuccessfully tried to withdraw their savings. Retired 80-year-old journalist Carlos Partcha stated:

"We don't trust anything anymore, not even the banking institutions... I had saved in dollars, and when the banks froze deposits in 2001, I got pesos back and lost my money."[44]

LIKE 2014 ENGLAND, US BANK RUNS ARE IMMINENT

When there is a threat of a bank run, banks freeze assets; otherwise, they would have no money left. As reported by the BBC (British Broadcasting Corporation), a number of HSBC customers were prevented from withdrawing larger sums because—and this is the disturbing part—

"They could not provide evidence of why they wanted it."[45, 46, 47]

MAJOR ISSUES WITH US BANKS BEGAN IN APRIL OF 2020

Today HSBC USA and Chase have instituted capital controls. Clients need to wait a minimum of five days before wiring funds to their own international accounts. This is the very nature of capital controls, which include restricting the free flow of capital (currency) across borders. The tactic causes people's currency to become trapped inside the controlling country that will no longer allow it to be exchanged for a better currency, thus forcing the citizens to keep holding the nation's rapidly devaluing currency.[48]
Right now America is experiencing a rising US dollar—but only relative to other currencies. This rise just means we are the least dilapidated financial house on a world block of homes that has been decimated. Our economic disaster is rapidly approaching and will be further fueled by the looming economic breakdown in Europe. Further evidence of American banks being in trouble has been seen in recent years with strange activity that appears to be about keeping them afloat:

SOMETHING IS REALLY WRONG!

SOURCE: St. Louis Fed, ING

Treasury general account   Reverse repo facility

For a couple years now, US banks have been unwilling to hold more European bank debt, even overnight. This is a bad sign for European banks, and again, their demise will also take down an already-teetering American banking system. The fates of most big banks around the world are tied to all the rest.

An increasing welfare state eventually causes nations to run out of money, resulting in restricted freedoms that lead to civil unrest and civilization collapse. In many ways the American welfare state parallels the ancient Romans' welfare state, both having piled up legions of beneficiaries (people living off the state), confiscatory taxation, burdensome regulation, and runaway inflation. And just like what happened with Rome, today's American battle has been made difficult to win because of our plummeting virtue, a loss of cultural character that does not tend to change until a nation hits rock bottom.

WHAT CAN WE DO?

American finances will get much worse before turning around, and we must never give up the fight for sound fiscal policy. There is hope in the reality that the Roman republic really never died: Italy still exists today and the United States continues to also. Our freedoms may be eroded, but we can thrive again—as God created us to do. Your mission is now to stay on guard through the storm, researching to understand the rapidly changing economic situation, taking steps to protect your family, helping others, and voting for fiscally responsible leadership.

Monumentally important through it all is to invest in tangible assets like gold and silver. As presidents, politicians, and dictators debase their currencies—to pay for entitlements and other government expansion—a family, society, and nation's only financial assurance will be tangible assets (as always). Protecting and preserving your savings is paramount. When banks start thinking your money is theirs, not letting you withdraw funds unless they approve of the use, you know trouble is right around the corner. It is too late by the time banks freeze assets and impose capital controls.

The writing is on the wall. America is following the same path as the Roman republic did, today debasing the US dollar to similarly ridiculous levels. Just like them, sometime soon

Americans will want out of the central banking system, but it will become increasingly difficult to do so because of ever-growing restrictions on withdrawals, freezing of accounts, and imposition of other capital controls. So take action now. Against worsening inflation, tangible assets like gold and silver will not only preserve and protect what you have worked for your entire life, but also function as barter when merchants no longer want the dollar in exchange for goods and services.

CHAPTER 9

HOW TO BEAT INFLATION

HOW INFLATION BEGINS

"Conspicuous consumption" (keeping up with the Joneses) happens as advancing technology creates a wealthier society, leading its people to strive toward the top of the social ladder. In 1934, Norwegian-American economist and sociologist Thorstein Veblen pointed out that some forms of consumption serve no purpose—other than to enhance social status.[49]

This sort of society-embraced hedonism becomes dangerous when the public appetite can no longer be satisfied by the people's current income. To maintain an elevated lifestyle, borrowing becomes the norm, something that always lowers the competitive position of the borrower. On a societal level, this decline into more and more utilization of cheap credit (low interest rates) offered on out-of-control money printing (mountains of cash put into society) is called *inflation*.

IMPLICATIONS OF INFLATION

As inflation persists and becomes excessive, the economy will eventually stagnate, producing increased interest rates, unemployment, and bankruptcies along with a collapsing standard of living and shortages in all types of essential and nonessential products. Increasing interest rates put downward pressure on many assets, including real estate, stocks, and bonds. Eventually investors try to get rid of their currency by exchanging it for anything tangible and liquid. From there the inflation rate can rapidly advance toward hyperinflation where savings accounts are eliminated and anyone living on a fixed income—like Social Security recipients—risk becoming impoverished almost overnight.

Because most nations today live under central banks that are uncontrollably printing their currency, this scenario is presently occurring all over the world at varying rates.

CAN IT HAPPEN IN AMERICA?

Of course it can. What I explained is simple economics, and America is *not* immune to universal laws of economics. But this process happens so slowly that the populace is unaware of the erosion in their purchasing power. Since the Federal Reserve was created in 1913, inflation has caused the dollar to lose 99% of its purchasing power.

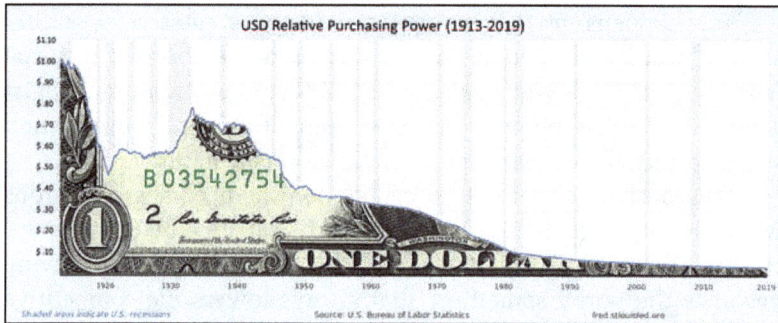

USD Relative Purchasing Power (1913-2019)

In 1913 dollars, today's dollar is only worth one cent, a deterioration that has been disguised by over one hundred years of devaluation—average Americans have taken little notice. The money-printing Federal Reserve might try to defend itself by pointing to rising wages over the same time period, but it never matches the loss of buying power. This is why we used to see only one working parent being able to feed and clothe an entire family. Now two are needed, even with smaller families. And these days that's not enough either: family borrowing has exploded, creating a society deeply in debt.[50]

INFLATION'S IMPLICATIONS TO DEMOCRACY

Imagine losing 99% of your life savings in a month, week, or even a day. That hyperinflationary scenario has happened many times in world history, from the Weimar Republic (1920s Germany) and 1990s Yugoslavia to Zimbabwe in the late 2000s and Venezuela beginning in 2016, plus countless others. During the hyperinflationary dance, both economic upheaval and social chaos crash the party—no one wants to be around for that.[51, 52, 53, 54]

HOW DOES IT END?

Economic shock and disorder normally lead to society accepting any reasonable solution that comes along, often meaning regime change from democracy to dictatorship, or vice versa. During the French Revolution, Napoleon came on the scene around 1800 and soon embarked on his Napoleonic Wars, which led to him dominating most of continental Europe. In 1920s Germany, Adolf Hitler arrived at the party, took over the dance floor, and eventually launched World War II. How did Hitler come to power? Well, during World War I, Germany inflicted massive physical and financial damage on its enemies. After the war's end, the 1919 Treaty of Versailles was signed, requiring Germany to pay for much of the rebuilding of nations and territories it destroyed. Having just gone through war themselves, the German people had little money, so they suddenly had a massive debt that was virtually impossible to pay back. This led to Germany abandoning the gold standard, allowing them to print currency without discretion. This devalued their currency to the point that no one wanted it, yet they just kept printing, and a snowball effect of *inflation* ensued.

Prior to Germany's hyperinflation that began in the second half of 1921, their currency had been relatively stable at about sixty German marks per US dollar. But when the inflation ball gets rolling, the deterioration can be devastatingly quick. Look at the rapid change in the number of German marks it took to buy just *one ounce* of gold.[55]

Jan 1919	170
Jan 1920	1,340
Jan 1921	1,349
Jan 1922	3,976
Jan 1923	372,447
May 1923	710,355
Oct 1923	1,347,070,000,000
Nov 1923	87,000,000,000,000

SOURCE: Kershaw, P. (1997). *Economic Solutions*. Boulder, CO: Heal our Land.

For people who have never experienced hyperinflation, these sorts of disastrous stories are hard to believe, but the scenario played out quickly in places like 1920s Germany where people had to pay for food with suitcases—and then wheelbarrows—of money. Even then, they would quickly part with their piles of cash before they would have to pay twice the amount. It was said that dinner goers had to negotiate the price of wine before the meal because it might be double by the end of their meal. Some Germans burned cash for warmth and dumped currency on the streets, but kept the more valuable basket it had been in.

Moms and dads could not feed their babies. People lost all hope. They were starving. Life was chaos. Enter Hitler. Like many politicians before and since, he promised hope and change, a message embraced by a desperate society. So, one of the most ruthless dictators the world has ever seen did not even have to hold a gun to people's heads; they willingly gave him the floor, and with it all their political, religious, personal, and economic freedom. They exchanged all that for *perceived*—but false—security. Again, that sort of unchecked inflation causes societies and nations to change from a democracy to a dictatorship.

Except for the early 1800s with Napoleon's unbacked francs (that were tied to French Revolutionary assignats which became worthless), every hyperinflationary period throughout history has occurred since 1914, and they were all because of fiat currencies (unbacked money printing). Before then, most currencies were backed by a nation's supply of gold or silver, which makes inflation almost impossible because it can only happen through a sudden increase to a country's pile of silver or gold. So inflation poses a direct threat to the kind of republic and wealth that are cherished in America.[56]

LET'S DEFINE A FEW TERMS

Deflation: a decrease in the money supply. Fewer dollars available to chase the same goods and services lead to decreased prices.

Inflation: an increase in the money supply. More dollars will bid up prices as the relative value of the currency decreases. It takes more of the "worth-*less*" currency to acquire the same goods and services.

Super-inflation: a double-digit inflation rate, not exceeding 100% per year.

Hyperinflation: definitions vary, but it begins at a rate either exceeding 100% per year or somewhere around 50% per month.

There are dozens of nations throughout history that have experienced hyperinflation. Here are a few:

Jan 1919	170
Jan 1920	1,340
Jan 1921	1,349
Jan 1922	3,976
Jan 1923	372,447
May 1923	710,355
Oct 1923	1,347,070,000,000
Nov 1923	87,000,000,000,000

WHAT CAUSES HYPERINFLATION?

The main cause is a massive increase in currency printed that's supported by corresponding growth in the nation's output of goods and services. This creates an imbalance between the supply and demand for money. When that rises to the level of hyperinflation, the situation effectively wipes out a currency's purchasing power. When a government decides to abandon any kind of tangible backing for their currency—whether gold, silver, oil, crops, and so on—the *only* value currency has is what the people are willing to attribute to it (until one day they don't).

A CLOSER LOOK INTO HYPERINFLATION

As inflation persists, the currency becomes more and more devalued, so investors must be *enticed* to invest in the nation, and that is done by raising interest rates. For example, let's say China sees that the United States is printing the US dollar like Monopoly money. Why would China want to invest in US Treasuries if the yield (interest rate) is only 2%? *They would not!* There must be an appropriate reward for the risk taken. To attract foreign investment, a country with an undesirable financial situation—and therefore a sketchy currency—needs to raise the interest rate it offers. Even a financially terrible country can attract investors if it pays 10% to 20% interest. But then that sort of high-interest debt causes more problems. If you think Monopoly money is a harsh characterization of today's American dollar printing, check out this parabolic chart of the US Monetary Base:

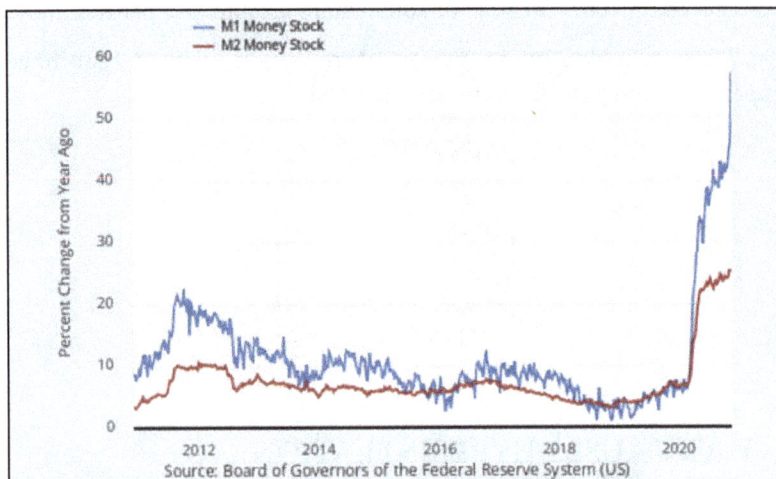

Source: Board of Governors of the Federal Reserve System (US)

Hyperinflation is coming!

HOW WILL HYPERINFLATION IMPACT YOUR LIFESTYLE?

1. Tangible-asset prices will go through the roof, and rising wages will *not* keep up, wiping out everyone not hedged (protected) by owning some tangible assets like physical gold and silver. Paper investments that claim to be linked to tangible assets—like the SLV and GLD ETFs (exchange-traded funds) for silver and gold— do not provide ironclad ownership, meaning you can lose any tangible asset that is not in your own possession or specifically stored in your name, separate from other people's metals.

2. This kind of economic tragedy will lead to a political revolution where the people generally lose personal, religious, economic, and political freedoms.

3. The currency will be decimated, leading to major trade imbalances with other nations. Whenever a debtor country—like the United States is right now—begins to default on its obligations, creditor nations become extremely upset. A downward cycle begins: financial problems lead to economic issues, which lead to political problems, which end as geopolitical issues like *war*!

Because America is already experiencing these eroding effects, the time to prepare is now!

HOW DO GOVERNMENTS TRY TO FIX THIS ONCE IT STARTS?

The initial government "fix" will make things worse: they print the currency like there is no tomorrow, hoping to stimulate the economy by providing liquidity—but that just brings more inflation. Running a deficit (spending more than we make) to the point of unsustainable debt has already led the government to run out of legitimate money, so the *only* ways out of this situation are to create more liquidity (print more money), try increasing revenue by raising taxes, or both. But those methods cause more inflation and raise taxes on people already financially stretched (they have personally borrowed too much). So raised taxes will mean people spend less, *lowering* government revenues. And prices rising at the same time people have reduced income (because of higher taxes) means disaster!

This sort of financial situation especially poses a problem for nations like the US that rely on a lot of imports. When the nations supplying the goods stop accepting US currency, people could starve. Then the 1920s Germany situation begins: political upheaval and civil unrest. Blood in the streets.

WHAT CAN WE DO?

Rightly anticipating a time when US dollars become worthless, you can start acquiring tangible products that will be useful for bartering (exchanging your goods or services for someone else's). Besides being phenomenal investments that act as a hedge against inflation, gold and silver can be great barter items because they are valuable and portable. In fact, they become extremely helpful during hyperinflation when their prices go through the roof; instead of just maintaining purchasing power, they actually increase in value as the purchasing power of the US dollar decreases.

Gold and silver always maintain their purchasing power: in the 1920s when the US dollar was still backed by gold, one ounce of gold was interchangeable with $20. Back then, either one would purchase a finely tailored men's suit, including the shirt, tie, belt, and shoes. What does $20 buy today? Only a low-quality tie. But that same ounce of gold is worth over $1000—which still buys the full men's suit.

In addition to being a fantastic investment, gold and silver are an insurance policy against a collapsing currency, especially today when the geopolitical and economic conditions all point toward gold and silver for preservation and protection. A minimum 50% allocation of your investable assets into precious metals will give you a 1:1 hedge against falling paper-asset value. But as the inflationary scenario becomes more extreme, putting an even higher percentage in tangible assets may be wise. A properly designed portfolio will also consist of high-quality, income-generating assets and an emergency cash fund.

In response to a devaluing currency, assets like stocks, bonds, mutual funds, and real estate get hit hard as interest rates go up, but gold and silver will also go up over time, thus minimizing your total portfolio risk, giving you much peace of mind in the midst of the storm.

And sometimes it *is* okay to have all your eggs in one basket, because diversification does not mean safety. Safety comes from being in the right place at the right time. Again, over-allocating into precious metals (more than 50% of your portfolio) may be prudent given our current economic conditions and where we are in the inflationary cycle. Precious metals give growth and insurance.

The goal of *all* investment portfolios is to be in the right place at the right time, following the positive trending asset classes. This minimizes risk and maximizes return. But the *wrong* thing to do is *doing nothing*! Also, stop taking advice from those you no longer trust. Insanity is when you keep doing the same thing over and over, expecting a different result. The obvious lesson of history is that the majority of people are moving in the wrong direction most of the time. So how is your present path? Just survival was not what you were created for. You can thrive. It's up to you. Take action now!

CHAPTER 10

PROTECTING YOUR IRA
WITH PRECIOUS METALS

Governments get crazy when they run out of money. Throughout history we see stories of countries that amassed mountains of debt, and it is always because the government spent more than their revenues. It's not rocket science. Just common sense. That's what happens. When families keep spending more than what is earned, they go bankrupt—and it works the same for nations. Overspending countries *will* eventually go bankrupt.

What should every family and nation do when faced with bankruptcy? Cut spending and increase revenues. But because governments have a printing press, they do not normally follow that sound advice; instead, they keep spending and even ramp it up, abandoning all financial responsibility. Each time a government prints more currency, they increase their money supply, devaluing their currency so that it takes more of the nation's money to purchase goods and services.

Here's a crucial concept that will change your view of the financial world: inflation is not some phenomenon where prices *mysteriously* rise. Inflation *is* rising prices, and it happens with *every* increase in the money supply.

As an example, consider that China manufactures televisions, cars, electronics—and seemingly everything else. The goods they produce have value, and they sell them to US companies. But what happens over time as we pay for their products with US dollars that we keep printing more and more of, even to the point today where we do so without discretion? While we furiously print more paper dollars that are backed by nothing tangible (to fund entitlements, stimulus programs, bailouts, and for giving away to governments around the world), other countries start to view the US dollar as Monopoly money. Chinese manufacturers would like us to stop the reckless printing because they provide valuable products that we keep paying for with junk currency. But we keep printing, so they continually require more and more of our devalued currency in exchange for their valuable products. They raise their prices on the goods and services they sell us.

That's inflation! Again, increased prices are just increased money supply, and as we saw in a M1 and M2 money-supply chart near the end of the last chapter, recent US currency injected into circulation has astronomically increased.

In 1971 President Richard Nixon took America off the gold standard, untying US dollars from any tangible-asset backing, allowing the government to print currency by fiat (decree)— however much they want. Politicians use their unlimited access to a printing press to buy votes, so the ever-increasing money printing has brought rising inflation, which means prices have gone up and up and up. Though it's not shocking to learn that a politician lied, the extent to which he did is astounding: When Nixon took us off the gold standard, he promised that our fiat currency would retain its full value. Instead, over the next 42 years the US dollar lost 99% of its value.[57]

WHY DOES ALL THIS MATTER TO YOUR FAMILY?

If your family's investments are not at least earning the rate of *unofficial* inflation—which is the real rate (not the government's *official* and false rate)—you will fall behind more and more every year. Though faultily calculated *official* US inflation had been below 5% since 2008, for May of 2022 it was reported as 8.3%, a rate you can find by looking at the government's Consumer Price Index (CPI). But again, that number is usually always much lower than the actual inflation rate called the *unofficial* rate.

As we discuss at length in chapter 5, the CPI measures the change in prices of a basket of goods over time. It is extremely flawed for political reasons.[58] Whenever a government can understate inflation, they save loads of money by allowing less of a payment increase than deserved by those receiving entitlement payouts—they cheat the recipients. As mentioned, the methodology used to calculate the government's CPI figures is invalid because they incorporate substitution, arithmetic versus geometric weighting, and quality adjustments. These aspects relegate the index to virtually useless information.

PHYSICAL PRECIOUS METALS FOR YOUR IRA

Most people do not realize that metals can be held as part of an IRA. This does include silver or gold mining shares, precious metals mutual funds, and metals ETFs, all of which are just paper assets. IRAs can purchase and hold physical gold and silver bars and coins. Physical precious metals are the safest way to own them. The Internal Revenue Service allows a government-approved list of metals that can be held in an IRA, as mentioned in the Taxpayer Relief Act of 1997.[59]

PUBLIC LAW 105–34—AUG. 5, 1997

TAXPAYER RELIEF ACT OF 1997

SEC. 304. CERTAIN BULLION NOT TREATED AS COLLECTIBLES.

(a) IN GENERAL.—Paragraph (3) of section 408(m) (relating to exception for certain coins) is amended to read as follows:
"(3) EXCEPTION FOR CERTAIN COINS AND BULLION.—For purposes of this subsection, the term 'collectible' shall not include—
"(A) any coin which is—
"(i) a gold coin described in paragraph (7), (8), (9), or (10) of section 5112(a) of title 31, United States Code,
"(ii) a silver coin described in section 5112(e) of title 31, United States Code,
"(iii) a platinum coin described in section 5112(k) of title 31, United States Code, or
"(iv) a coin issued under the laws of any State, or
"(B) any gold, silver, platinum, or palladium bullion of a fineness equal to or exceeding the minimum fineness that a contract market (as described in section 7 of the Commodity Exchange Act, 7 U.S.C. 7) requires for metals which may be delivered in satisfaction of a regulated futures contract,
if such bullion is in the physical possession of a trustee described under subsection (a) of this section.".
(b) EFFECTIVE DATE.—The amendment made by this section shall apply to taxable years beginning after December 31, 1997.   26 USC 408 note.

SOURCE:
(http://www.gpo.gov/fdsys/pkg/PLAW-105publ34/pdf/PLAW-105publ34.pdf)

The kinds of precious metals you can own in an IRA are gold, gold proofs, silver, platinum, and palladium.

GOLD

Those pictured below are the most popular types of gold bullion coins owned in IRAs. Also allowed are other Austrian gold coins and COMEX or NYMEX (Commodity Exchange or New York Mercantile Exchange) approved bars and rounds. The bullion coins come in many sizes like 1 ounce, 0.50 ounce, 0.25 ounce, and 0.10 ounce.

AMERICAN EAGLE   CANADIAN MAPLE LEAF   AUSTRIAN PHILHARMONIC

AMERICAN EAGLE GOLD PROOFS

American eagle gold-proof coins are a more collectible version of the gold eagle coin. The precise engraving and frosted images that appear to float above the mirror-like background enhance the intrinsic beauty of these designs. The cameo effect is made possible by specifically treated, hand-polished dies. The blanks (faceless rounds) are struck multiple times to ensure the highest relief possible. Because these coins are such a small percentage of all gold eagles minted, they sell for a premium over the price of regular bullion gold eagles.

Based on supply and demand, the added premium for gold proofs often expands and contracts with market conditions. Many dealers increase their promotion of these coins during times of low coin premiums. They claim the coins can offer the advantage of multiplied growth, potentially rising in both spot price and premium expansion. While they *may*, during my 27 years in the industry, I have rarely seen this result.

SILVER

Available silver options to be owned in an IRA are American eagles, Canadian maple leafs, Mexican libertads, and COMEX-approved bars and rounds:

AMERICAN EAGLE   CANADIAN MAPLE LEAF   COMEX APPROVED BAR

PLATINUM

Available options for an IRA are platinum American eagles, Canadian maple leafs, Isle of Man noble coins, and NYMEX-approved bars and rounds.

PLATINUM AMERICAN EAGLE   PLATINUM MAPLE LEAF   PLATINUM BAR

PALLADIUM

Available IRA options are palladium bars and coins.

PALLADIUM MAPLE LEAF   PALLADIUM BAR

FREQUENTLY ASKED QUESTIONS

Can I take custody of my IRA assets? No. All IRA assets must remain within the custody of a custodian or trustee of the IRA. You may take a distribution of your assets from your IRA, but it is a taxable event reported to the IRS. In that case, unless you make a qualified rollover contribution of the assets into another plan, you will probably owe income taxes on the value of the distribution and are likely to also be subject to a penalty for performing a premature distribution. As always, consult with your investment advisor regarding these matters.

What is a self-directed IRA? It is like any other IRA except for one major difference: you get to choose where your IRA funds will be invested, rather than just accepting whatever the IRA trustee or custodian offers. This gives you greater flexibility because you can choose precious metals, stocks, bonds, CDs, mutual funds, government obligations, or other investments.

How do I move my existing IRA to a new custodian so I can fund it with precious metals? Money in an existing IRA can be moved to a new custodian by either a transfer or rollover. A transfer does not require IRS reporting, and there are no restrictions on how often you can transfer funds. Your new custodian will contact the previous institution and take care of getting the funds moved. Special rules apply if you have reached the age of 70½, so you should check with your present trustee or custodian to see if there will be fees or penalties.

Can I contribute bullion or coins I already own into a self-directed IRA? No. All contributions must be made in cash except in the case of transfers or rollovers.

What is the difference between a traditional IRA and a Roth IRA? Anyone who has earned income can contribute to an IRA each year. Depending on your income, marital status, and participation in an employer's plan, your contribution to a traditional IRA may be tax deductible. Contributions to a Roth IRA are never tax deductible, but qualified distributions to you from your Roth account come out completely tax free. So, if you start with $5000 in your Roth and it grows to $50,000 over the decades, none of that $45,000 increase is taxed. With a traditional IRA, if your $5000 contribution goes in tax deductible, you will be taxed on the increased $45,000 as distributions are taken. Non-deductible contributions grow tax-free in a Roth IRA and only tax-deferred in a traditional IRA. This tax-favored treatment usually makes even a non-deductible Roth contribution a smart move. Your tax advisor can help you determine which type of IRA is most appropriate for you.

My bank IRA is free, so why is there a fee for my self-directed IRA? A bank has its fee built into the interest rate it pays you, and that bank will probably not allow you to invest in precious metals. Since the custodian holding the precious metals receives no commission from any of your investment actions, separate fees are necessary to cover the cost of maintenance and storage.

How much will an IRA denominated in precious metals cost me per year? It is cheaper than you might think, and the majority of the fee is for storage. Since you are purchasing a specific pile of physical metals for your account, they need to be safely stored. The fees should range from $200 to $300 annually, regardless of the amount of metal in your account.

When I qualify for a distribution, may I receive the coins instead of a check? Yes. These "in-kind" distributions are permitted. However, upon distribution you will have to pay ordinary income tax on the metals or cash that you receive—for the year you receive it.

What specific types of precious metals are permitted in my IRA?

○   American gold, silver, and platinum eagle coins

○   Austrian philharmonic coins

○   Australian kangaroos, nuggets, kookaburras, and koala coins

○   Silver Mexican libertads

○   Platinum Isle of Man noble coins

○   Gold bars and rounds manufactured by a NYMEX- or COMEX-approved refiner/assayer (and meeting minimum fineness requirements of 0.999+)

○   Silver bars and rounds manufactured by a COMEX-approved refiner/assayer (and meeting minimum fineness requirements of 0.9995+)

○   Palladium bars and rounds manufactured by a NYMEX-approved refiner/assayer (and meeting minimum fineness requirements of 0.9995+)

How will the coins be physically stored? When the coins arrive at the storage facility, the shipment will be opened in order to inspect the contents, which will then be resealed in the same shipping box and placed in the vault. This ensures the coins acquired on your behalf are the exact ones stored as yours.

Can my current IRS custodian, bank, or broker help me set up an IRA in precious metals? More than likely the answer is *no*. The only precious metals IRA that most brokers and banks can set up are generally invested in paper gold stocks and mutual funds which are considerably riskier and more speculative.

How safe is the storage facility? Our selected custodians utilize one of the oldest and largest private storage facilities in the country. The coins are insured and remain locked in the safest possible environment.

Can I sell my precious metals in the future and transfer or roll over the proceeds into another type of IRA? Yes. At some point in the future, you may choose to take profits on your precious metals holdings and transfer them into stocks, bonds, CDs, or any other types of investments that are allowed in IRAs.

CHAPTER 11

STATE PENSIONS FACING INSOLVENCY

When state pensions in America reach insolvency, what will happen to the retirement assets of those living in the bankrupt states, and what remedy does the federal government have that states do not? This chapter will address the first question, and the answer to the second is a printing press, which is why most countries around the world do not have a balanced budget. If there is ever a national shortfall, countries have the option of printing their way out of it, but only when their currency has no tangible backing—when it is just a paper promise.

When states run out of money, the residents—especially state employees—pay the price. States rely on taxes, fees, and tolls to bring in revenue, but they have no currency-printing press like the federal government. If a state runs out of money, they have to institute austerity measures like cutting services and delaying benefits. Another option for a state is to try increasing revenue through higher taxes.

Today many US states have a financial crisis unfolding, and the outcome will inevitably involve state pension funds becoming insolvent. This means state employees who have been expecting fruitful retirements are in for a rude awakening.

STATE PENSIONS STUDY

In 2010 Dr. Joshua D. Rauh from the Finance Department at Northwestern University's Kellogg School of Management conducted research on the sustainability of public-sector state pensions. His research results shown in the chart below project the year each state pension fund will run out of assets, assuming they earn 8% each year on their assets and use future contributions to fully fund future benefits. Another study assumption is that each state's pension fund will see increased revenue of 3% per year. The last column in the chart shows the actual rate of return seen in 2020, and the interest earned for every state was below the 8% assumption, meaning the funds will have even less for assets than what the study assumed. Since around 1983, the US government has implemented a policy of pursuing lower and lower interest rates, so this chart's reveal of the low 2020 interest earned and Rauh's original insolvency projections are not surprising:

STATE	Year of insolvency (8% returns)	Actual Return 2020	STATE	Year of insolvency (8% returns)	Actual Return 2020
Illinois	2018	4.6%	Vermont	2028	4%
Connecticut	2019	1.86%	Arizona	2029	.5%
Indiana	2019	2.56%	Arkansas	2030	2.4%
New Jersey	2019	1.21%	California	2030	4.7%
Hawaii	2020	1.26%	Ohio	2030	2.96%
Louisiana	2020	0.27%	Wyoming	2030	NR
Oklahoma	2020	4.5%	South Dakota	2031	1.6%
Colorado	2022	-0.80%	Nebraska	2032	2.2%
Kansas	2022	2.1%	Virginia	2033	1.4%
Kentucky	2022	1.2%	Washington	2033	3.71%
New Hampshire	2022	1.1%	Delaware	2035	0.50%
Alabama	2023	NR	Iowa	2035	3.4%
Michigan	2023	0.10%	Tennessee	2035	4.9%
Minnesota	2023	4.2%	Utah	2036	NR
Mississippi	2023	3.4%	Texas	2037	-3.3%
Maryland	2024	3.6%	Wisconsin	2038	4.7%
Pennsylvania	2024	-4.58%	Oregon	2039	0.52%
South Carolina	2024	1.6%	North Dakota	2041	3.46%
West Virginia	2024	2.2%	Idaho	2043	2.80%
Missouri	2025	5.2%	Georgia	2047	5.42%
Maine	2026	1.8%	Alaska	-	3.83%
Massachusetts	2026	2.4%	Florida	-	2.58%
New Mexico	2026	-1.5%	Nevada	-	7.20%
Montana	2027	2.68%	New York	-	-2.68%
Rhode Island	2027	3.8%	North Carolina	-	4.4%

Today the underfunding of state pensions is at the all-time high of $1.34 trillion, reflecting extremely excessive state liabilities (for present and future payments) compared to expected assets.

A LEGALIZED PONZI SCHEME?

Over 30 million Americans were unemployed during 2020, which meant none of them paid into state pension funds, though all these state programs require working contributors to pay past contributors who are now retired and receiving payments—it's like a legalized Ponzi scheme. Cooked into the pension soup is the understanding that more and more workers will age and retire until the ultimately top-heavy pension plan will have more retirees receiving benefits than the younger population that is working and paying into the system. Again, it's a Ponzi scheme.

STRUCTURAL CH1ANGES IN THE US ECONOMY

Demographic changes for nations will also have a lasting impact. The fertility rate in the United States has fallen below two for the first time ever. In chapter 8, I go into detail on the ramifications. Again, when the fertility rate is below two, meaning the average two adults replace themselves with less than two children, the population shrinks. Countries now with fertility rates below two include the US, most other western economies, and industrialized Asia.

ENTITLEMENTS AT RISK

An even deeper and wider problem than the state-employee-pension funds is America's issue with the federal entitlement system. With a lesser percentage of the population working and paying into the system than in previous generations, the US economy could crash anytime now. As more and more of the baby boomer generation (those born from 1946 to 1964) reach retirement years—where they stop paying in and start receiving money back—an inadequate number of working-age Americans is creating a revenue crisis that will inevitably kill the economy.

As detailed in chapter 8, the Roman republic fell when just a third of all revenues were going to feed their welfare state, compared to America's financial situation in 2022 where 96.2% of all federal tax revenue will go to entitlements like Social Security, Medicare, Medicaid, food stamps, WIC, and other programs. Technically, Social Security is not an entitlement because we all pay into it our entire lives in exchange for retirement income, but like entitlements the Social Security benefits cannot be taken away easily; it is a fairly set liability against US government revenues.

Proposed Budget by Category
(In billions of dollars)

	2020	2021	2022	2023	2024	2025	2026	2027	2028	2029	2030	2031	2022-2026	2022-2031
Outlays:														
Discretionary programs:														
Defense	714	735	756	756	775	791	804	816	826	835	843	851	3,881	8,052
Non-defense	913	960	932	930	909	914	917	927	947	964	984	1,002	4,601	9,426
Subtotal, discretionary programs	1,627	1,696	1,688	1,685	1,683	1,704	1,721	1,743	1,773	1,799	1,827	1,854	8,482	17,478
Mandatory programs:														
Social Security	1,090	1,135	1,196	1,261	1,333	1,410	1,492	1,579	1,672	1,767	1,866	1,966	6,691	15,542
Medicare	769	709	766	841										
Medicaid	458	52	571	582										
Other mandatory programs	2,260	2,885	1,486	1,324										
Subtotal, mandatory programs	4,578	5,251	4,018	4,008										
Net interest	345	303	305	320										
Total outlays	6,550	7,249	6,011	6,013	6,187	6,508	6,746	6,935	7,312	7,425	7,847	8,211	31,465	69,196
Receipts:														
Individual income taxes	1,609	1,705	2,039	2,242	2,288	2,436	2,676	2,896	3,044	3,194	3,354	3,526	11,680	27,694
Corporation income taxes	212	268	371	577	649	673	664	666	679	678	681	693	2,933	6,330
Social insurance and retirement receipts:														
Social Security payroll taxes	965	944	1,033	1,072	1,118	1,159	1,207	1,252	1,311	1,361	1,417	1,474	5,587	12,403
Medicare payroll taxes	292	287	359	383	400	418	436	453	476	496	518	540	1,995	4,478
Unemployment insurance	43	55	59	61	60	57	55	55	57	56	58	56	293	576
Other retirement	10	10	11	12	12	13	13	14	15	16	17	17	62	140
Excise taxes	87	74	84	89	93	94	95	96	96	98	101	102	455	948
Estate and gift taxes	18	18	21	18										
Customs duties	69	85	57	45										
Deposits of earnings, Federal Reserve System	82	97	103											
Other miscellaneous receipts	36	37	39	40										
Total receipts	3,421	3,580	4,174	4,641										
Deficit:	3,129	3,669	1,837	1,372										
Net interest	345	303	305	320										
Primary deficit	2,784	3,366	1,532	1,052										
On-budget deficit	3,142	3,595	1,789	1,301	1,264	1,341	1,260	1,115	1,205	1,045	1,174	1,223	6,956	12,718
Off-budget deficit/surplus (−)	−13	73	48	71	95	129	154	189	219	262	303	345	496	1,813

Annotations overlaid on the table:
- TOTAL SOCIAL SECURITY, MEDICARE, MEDICAID, and MANDATORY PAYMENTS: $4.02T +$305B
- MANDATORY PAYMENTS: $4.32T
- Interest=$4.32T
- TOTAL FEDERAL REVENUE $4.17T
- ENTITLEMENTS + MANDATORY PAYMENTS = 96% of FED REVENUE
- ADD INTEREST ON OUR NATIONAL DEBT + ENTITLEMENTS AND MANDATORY PAYMENTS = 103% of FED REVENUE

So ancient Rome collapsed under a third of revenues going towards entitlement programs, and the US is at 96.2%—a completely unsustainable number. That means an imminent crash! In fact, our total spending for 2022 is projected to be a bit over $6 trillion, when our federal government will only bring in revenue of a little over $4 trillion. Part of that spending includes 2% net interest on the national debt, costing us a whopping $305 billion. But right now, we have the lowest sustained interest rates in history, so our massive debt will become even more devastating as interest rates inevitably rise from ground level. Consider what the net interest on our $30.5 trillion of federal debt will be when interest rates move up to more historical norms like these:

4% = $1.2 trillion per year

6% = $1.8 trillion per year

8% = $2.4 trillion per year

When interest rates reach just 3%, it and entitlements will cost us more than revenues. And interest rates are cyclical, changing long-term direction about every 28 years. In 1983, interest rates were 18% before beginning to move lower. Almost 40 years later, we have been seeing extremely low rates for many years. So our present low rates are well past when the average cycle should turn back up—and we can only go up from here.

So America is becoming insolvent along with state pension funds. When we consider the official federal budget with massive expenditures well over present revenues, the US is poised for default unless we continue to increase money printing. But that is leading to hyperinflation, which will decimate the wealth, standard of living, and livelihood of Americans who do not own enough tangible assets.

HOW CAN OUR STATE AND FEDERAL GOVERNMENTS FIX THE PROBLEM?

Well, a balanced budget amendment is out of the question because there are only three ways to accomplish that—increased revenue, decreased expenditures, or a combination of both—and America already has over 80% of our expenditures going to entitlements or other mandatory payments that are almost impossible to reduce. But something has to give. Options include implementing austerity measures that lower benefits and make them more difficult to receive, changing the age at which benefits become available, or eliminating them altogether. It is easy for money-printing politicians to increase benefits in their efforts to buy more votes, but once any entitlement has been dished out, lack of political will makes it almost impossible to take back any benefits without incurring some sort of citizen revolt.

TOO LITTLE TOO LATE?

The alternative is to try increasing revenues. In America today this cannot be done by increasing taxes because most Americans are living at the margin financially. When tax rates are increased while people still have plenty of disposable income, tax payers continue spending, which means total government revenues increase. However, with the vast majority of Americans stretched financially, raising taxes takes away crucial income that will cause the population to decrease spending, thus lowering government revenue from sales and income taxes.

CREATE JOBS

Another way to fix a revenue shortfall is by bringing jobs back to the US. We need to get more Americans working again, generating revenue through valuable services or creating products the world wants. A combination of monetary- and fiscal-policy adjustments would help create more jobs. Some of those job-supporting changes would include putting more tariffs on foreign goods, weakening the

US dollar, and reducing government red tape. These steps increase exports and decrease imports. Before America implemented so many government taxes, it used to make most of the money it spends through tariffs—other countries that liked our products would pay to fund US and state governments through tariffs.

TAKE ADVANTAGE OF THE TRENDS

With state pensions facing insolvency and our federal government set to quickly run out of money, you can take business and individual actions to take advantage of these trends, rather than let the trends continue taking advantage of you. Now is the time to act, making structural changes to your company, financial portfolio, and way of life—and that starts with decreasing your reliance on paper promises from broke governments and increasing tangible assets.

REFERENCES

○ Brown, Jeffrey R., & David W. Wilcox. (2009). Discounting state and local pension liabilities. *American Economic Review, 99*(2), 538–542.

○ Munnell, Alicia H., Haverstick, Kelly, Sass, Steven, & Aubry, Jean-Pierre. (2008). The miracle of funding by state and local pension plans. Center for Retirement Research at Boston College, issue in Brief #5.

○ Randazzo, A., and Moody, J. (2020). State of pensions 2020. Equable Institute: New York, NY.

○ Rauh, Joshua D. (2010). Are state public pensions sustainable? Why the federal government should worry about state pension liabilities. *National Tax Journal, (63)*3.

○ Novy-Marx, Robert, & Rauh, Joshua D. (2011). Public pension promises: How big are they and what are they worth? *The Journal of Finance, (66)*4, 1211–1249.

CHAPTER 12

ENGAGING THE CULTURE IN A TIME OF CONFLICT

How can we find peace in the midst of an economic tsunami? First, we must get prepared by investing in tangible assets that have been *the* proven way to protect wealth for millennia. And this will only continue, as demonstrated by today's central banks—the ones with most of the money—which have been loading up on gold to survive in the current and future financial crisis. They know it is headed for economic disaster.

Second, no matter the battle, storm, war, accident, political fight, or contentious financial transaction, continue thriving by doing as the Bible tells us: God's two most important commandments are to love the Lord and love others—in that order and above all else. We must be the peacemakers, especially in these days of drive-by slandering on social media. Wherever you or I see more sour seeds being sown to create greater animosity and division, we must be the rock others can cling to. Don't add to the division; instead, maintain and spread love, even during disagreement.

This was the godly advice put to work by some World War I soldiers who were living in cold, damp trenches. Soon followed by others, one brave peacemaker started something special on a Christmas Eve over 100 years ago. For context around that story, here's a summary of how World War I began:

THE HISTORICAL IMPORTANCE OF ARCHDUKE FRANZ FERDINAND OF AUSTRIA[60]

In 1889, Franz Ferdinand's life changed dramatically. His cousin Crown Prince Rudolf committed suicide at Rudolf's hunting lodge, which left Franz Ferdinand's father Karl Ludwig as first in line to the Austrian throne. Karl died of typhoid fever in 1896, and Ferdinand was then groomed for succession to lead his nation.

IMAGE: Smithsonian Magazine
https://www.smithsonianmag.com/history/curses-archduke-franz-ferdinand-and-his-astounding-death-car-27881052/

SPINNING OUT OF CONTROL

Then in 1914, Archduke Ferdinand was assassinated on June 28, which sparked a global conflict that led Austria to declare war on Serbia July 28. To help Serbia, Russia declared war on Austria the same day. Germany then declared war with Russia on August 1 and France on August 3. The same day, France declared war on Germany, and Germany on Belgium. The next day Britain declared war on Belgium and Germany. Two days later Austria declared war on Russia.[61, 62]

Because a royal guy got killed, 20 million more people lost their lives in World War I. Why did so many die in that war when the world had a much smaller population? It was from trench warfare, a brutal military tactic—extremely deadly.

IMAGE: Shutterstock

The idea with trench warfare is to establish a position, dig yourself in, and hide there so you *never* show up in the gunsights of your enemies; you just hold firm to your established position and hurl a lot of explosives at the other side's trenches.

Over the four years of WWI, the battle lines did not move much, accomplishing little. Neither geography nor national leaders changed, but a lot of people died.

AN AMAZING CHRISTMAS EVE!

Only six months into "the Great War," one brave soul got into the spirit of the season and decided to climb out of his trench without a weapon. The man stepped toward the enemy (into no man's land between the warring positions) and began loudly declaring a ceasefire. Soon others joined him from both sides, and that became the Christmas Truce of 1914.[63, 64, 65]

A HIDDEN KEY TO OUR FUTURE

Even though the nations at war disagreed on so much, that day the British, German, and French soldiers focused on what they had in common—being Christians who wanted to celebrate Christmas. This realization caused them to look each other in the eye, talk, experience a reprieve, eat together, even play some sports, and savor peace in the midst of the storm, while their weapons laid on the ground.

RELATIONSHIP CHANGES EVERYTHING

That night changed the men involved; so much so, the next day when fighting resumed many of them could not attack those they had just been eating with and enjoying time with. The commanding officers had to reassign the men to a different front because those peacemakers simply could not attack men they had become friendly with. Because that experience taught the leadership that people most likely won't kill those they know and like, in the years that followed a new military rule was established: "No fraternization with the enemy."

MODERN-DAY TRENCH WARFARE

Fast forward to today when social media has created a sort of online trench warfare, where someone takes a stand on an issue that they have read or heard about. From that they establish a position and—without knowing the full story or often not having met the other people—they begin firing ammo at all who disagree. And our modern technology even allows social media companies to fuel the fighting with millions of fake bot accounts that support social media leadership's side—normally the globalist view.

SOCIAL MEDIA SHOWS NATIONS DIVIDED

The divisions we see today stem from politics, race, gender, class, nationality, religion, marriage, and many other areas of society. Modern people are looking for division rather than commonality, and they do not want to change. Instead they constantly add to their pile of ammo so they can continue the relentless attack on people that have a different opinion—often assuming all opposed are deeply and personally *against* each other.

This problem is monumentally concerning, and someone

must be courageous to take that first step out of the trenches and enter no man's land, bringing a bold message of the need to find commonality and relationship. In the spirit of those brave, loving men during Christ's birthday in 1914, we all must be willing to drop our weapons and focus on what unites rather than divides us, ending our own internal war stance so that the external war can be reconciled. Resolving a conflict just means settling it, though the two parties may continue in their animosity toward each other. But to reconcile is to restore—or forge—friendly relations. Of course the latter is much preferred for contented coexistence. Dr. Martin Luther King, Jr., explained it this way:

> *"Darkness cannot drive out darkness: only light can do that. Hate cannot drive out hate: only love can do that."*

Likewise, only by shining the light of truth on our current individual, national, and global financial situation—and then taking the necessary steps to safeguard family savings—can we *end* up *Thriving in the Economic Tsunami.*

Kirk Elliott PhD

Private Advisors can be reached at (720) 605-3900, or visit our website at *KirkElliottPhD.com*

REFERENCES

1. https://www.federalreserve.gov/newsevents/pressreleases/files/
    bcreg20201209a1.pdf
2. https://wolfstreet.com/2021/06/17/holy-moly-feds-reverse-repos-spike-to-
    756-billion-undoing-6-months-of-qe-in-opposite-direction-feds-qe-pushes-
    assets-past-8-trillion/
3. https://fred.stlouisfed.org/series/RRPONTSYD
4. https://tradingeconomics.com/commodity/baltic
5. Elliott, K. (2007, 2013): "An Empirical Identification of an Appropriate
    Inflation Definition and an Inflation-Targeting Monetary Policy." Colorado:
    Today's America
6. https://www.bloomberg.com/news/articles/2022-01-12/inflation-in-u-s-
    registers-biggest-annual-gain-since-1982
7. https://www.bls.gov/news.release/cpi.t01.htm
8. https://www.macrotrends.net/2521/30-year-treasury-bond-rate-yield-chart
9. https://www.goodreads.com/quotes/108530-a-democracy-cannot-exist-as-a-
    permanent-form-of-government
10. https://laffercenter.org/about/curve/
11. https://fred.stlouisfed.org/series/MABMM301USM189S
12. https://www.cnbc.com/2022/08/18/russia-offers-mother-heroine-medal-
    and-16800-for-having-10-children.html
13. https://www.bankrate.com/banking/cds/historical-cd-interest-
    rates-1984-2016/
14. https://www.forecast-chart.com/rate-cd-interest.html
15. https://fred.stlouisfed.org/series/DGS10
16. https://www.multpl.com/10-year-treasury-rate/table/by-month
17. https://www.marketwatch.com/investing/index/djia
18. https://fred.stlouisfed.org/series/MSPUS
19. https://www.gold.org/data/gold-price
20. https://silverprice.org/silver-price-history.html
21. Baumohl, B. (2005). The secrets of economic indicators. Upper Saddle
    River, NJ: Wharton School Publishing.
22. Boskin, M. J., Dulberger, E. R., Gordon, R. J., Griliches, Z., & Jorgenson, D.
    (1996). Toward a more accurate measure of the cost of living. Retrieved
    April 7, 2006, from
23. Griliches, Z. (1967). Hedonic price indexes revisited: some notes on the
    state of the art. Proceedings of the business and economic statistics
    section, American Statistical Association, 324–332.

24. Krumme, G., & Hayter, R. (1975). Implications of corporate strategies and product cycle adjustments for regional employment changes. In Collins & Walker (Eds.), The dynamics of manufacturing activity (pp. 325–356). New York: Wiley.
25. Malecki, E. J. (1991). Technology and economic development: The dynamics of local, regional, and national change. New York: Wiley.
26. Rosen, S. (1974). Hedonic prices and implicit markets: Product differentiation in pure competition. Journal of Political Economy, 82(Jan/Feb), 34–55.
27. Wasson, C. R. (1974). Dynamic competitive strategy and product cycles. St. Charles, IL: Challenge Books.
28. Welling, K. M. (2006). Shadowing reality. Welling@Weeden, (8)4. Greenwich, CT: Weeden & Co., L.P.
29. Williams, W. J. (2004). The consumer price index. Government economic reports: Things you've suspected but were afraid to ask! Retrieved April 18, 2006, from
30. https://dictionary.reference.com/browse/currency
31. Reed, Lawrence. "The Fall of Rome and Modern Parallels" https://www.youtube.com/watch?v=FPFlH6eGqsg
32. https://en.wikipedia.org/wiki/Virtus_(virtue)
33. https://www.cato.org/sites/cato.org/files/pubs/pdf/the_work_versus_welfare_trade-off_2013_wp.pdf
34. https://www.brainyquote.com/quotes/alexander_hamilton_386596
35. https://www.fee.org/the_freeman/detail/the-fall-of-rome-and-modern-parallels#axzz2sHPPoqou
36. Reflections on the Revolution in France, a political pamphlet written by the Irish statesman Edmund Burke and published in November 1790
37. https://www.examiner.com/article/socialist-venezuela-business-forced-to-lower-prices-to-be-fair-or-face-arrest
38. https://en.mercopress.com/2013/10/11/venezuela-inflation-soars-to-49-maduro-promises-more-dollars-to-help-with-imports
39. https://www.financialsense.com/contributors/steve-hanke/venezuela-hyperinflation
40. https://www.financialsense.com/sites/default/files/users/u2228/images/2013/venezuela-inflation.png
41. https://www.examiner.com/article/socialist-venezuela-business-forced-to-lower-prices-to-be-fair-or-face-arrest
42. https://www.nzherald.co.nz/business/news/article.cfm?c_id=3&objectid=11195755
43. https://www.reuters.com/article/2014/01/31/us-argentina-currency-analysis-idUSBREA0U1GG20140131

44. https://www.bloomberg.com/news/2014-01-30/the-price-of-argentina-s-devaluation.html

45. https://www.naturalnews.com/043762_bank_runs_restrictions_HSBC.html

46. https://www.bbc.co.uk/news/business-25861717

47. https://dailycaller.com/2014/01/29/bank-refuses-to-give-customers-their-money-unless-they-can-prove-a-good-reason-for-needing-it/

48. https://www.economicpolicyjournal.com/2013/10/shock-hsbc-usa-joins-chase-in-limiting.html

49. Veblen, T. (1934). The theory of the leisure class: an economic study of institutions with a foreword by Stuart Chase. New York: The Modern Library.

50. Bresciani-Turroni, C. (1937/2003). The economics of inflation. (Sayers, Trans.). London: Routledge.

51. Parsson, J. O. (1974). Dying of money. Boston: Wellspring Press.

52. Ringer, F. K. (Ed.). (1969). The German inflation of 1923. New York: Oxford University Press.

53. Smith, A. (1963). An inquiry into the nature and causes of the wealth of nations with an introduction by M. Blaug (Vol. II). Homewood, IL: Richard D. Irwin, Inc.

54. Kershaw, P. (1997). Economic solutions. Boulder, CO: Heal Our Land Ministries.

55. Bernholz, P. (2003). Monetary regimes and inflation. Northampton, MA: Edward Elgar Publishing.

56. https://www.foxbusiness.com/politics/federal-reserve-bank-minneapolis-ceo-inflation-very-concerning-spreading-across-economy

57. https://www.resourceinvestor.com/2011/01/24/is-this-time-different-for-the-dollar

58. https://data.bls.gov/timeseries/CUUR0000SA0?output_view=pct_12 mths

59. https://www.gpo.gov/fdsys/pkg/PLAW-105publ34/pdf/PLAW-105publ34.pdf

60. https://www.smithsonianmag.com/history/curses-archduke-franz-ferdinand-and-his-astounding-death-car-27381052/

61. ttps://guides.loc.gov/chronicling-america-wwi-declarations

62. http://www.history.com/this-day-in-history/first-world-war-erupts-in-europe

63. https://www.smithsonianmag.com/history/the-story-of-the-wwi-christmas-truce-11972213/

64. https://www.history.com/topics/world-war-i/christmas-truce-of-1914

65. https://www.washingtonpost.com/news/retropolis/wp/2017/12/24/the-christmas-truce-miracle-soldiers-put-down-their-guns-to-sing-carols-and-drink-wine/

www.ingramcontent.com/pod-product-compliance
Lightning Source LLC
Chambersburg PA
CBHW060932220326
41597CB00020BA/3720